Peaks of Glory

CLIMBING THE WORLD'S HIGHEST MOUNTAINS

CHARTWELL
BOOKS, INC.

Contents

Text by
Stefano Ardito

Edited by
Valeria Manferto
Laura Accomazzo

Designed by
Patrizia Balocco

Translated by
Antony Shugaar

The publisher would like to thank the following people for their help in making this volume possible:
Jeff Achey of *Climbing Magazine*, Carbondale, Colorado; Jean Michel Asselin of *Vertical*, Grenoble, France; Chris Baxter of *Wild*, Prahran, Victoria, Australia; Fran Botha of *Southern Rock*, Saxonworld, South Africa; Barrie Cook of *New Zealand Alpine Journal*, Wellington, New Zealand; Sandro Parisotto, Sieghard Pircher, and Jean Marc Porte of *Montagnes Magazine*, Meylan, France; Robert Schaller, Jr. and Camilla Valletti of *Alp*, Turin, Italy.

Special thanks go to Roberto Mantovani of *La Rivista della Montagna*, Turin, Italy.

Published in 2001 by
CHARTWELL BOOKS, INC.
A Division of
BOOK SALES, INC.
114 Northfield Avenue
Edison, New Jersey 08837

New extended and up-dated edition

*First published by
Edizioni White Star.
Title of the original edition:
Cime di gloria, immagini
e racconti del grande alpinismo
World copyright*
© 1993, 2001 White Star s.r.l.

ISBN: 0-7858-1369-1

Printed in Italy

PAGE 1 A climber descends into a blizzard along the Abruzzi Spur on K2 during the American expedition of 1990. Photograph by Greg Child

PAGES 2-3 A freshly-fallen snow impedes a climber on the southwest slope of Gasherbrum II in the Karakoram Range. Photograph by Mark Buscail

PAGES 4-5 A climber nears the summit of Cerro Torre, the symbol of mountaineering in Patagonia.

Photograph by Maurizio Giordani

PAGE 6 Mountain climber and photographer Galen Rowell pauses during a storm on the west ridge of Everest during the 1983 expedition. Photograph by John Roskelley

PAGE 7 During the American expedition of 1978, Rick Ridgeway, foreground, climbs a wall on the Chinese slope of K2. Photograph by John Roskelley

PAGES 8-9 In 1986, Alison Hargreaves takes a break just below the peak of Kangtega, which rises 22,241 feet over Nepal. Photograph by Marc F. Twight/Agence Freestyle

PAGES 10-11 The imposing silhouette of Nuptse catches the light of sunset. Photograph by Toni Hiebler/ Bavaria

PAGES 12-13 Christophe Profit climbs toward an ice overhang on the south wall of Lhotse during an

attempt in the fall of 1990. Photograph by Pierre Béghin

PAGES 14-15 A team approaches Camp II during a climb up Gasherbrum II. Photograph by Mark Buscail

PAGES 16-17 Climbers scale the Kuffner Ridge on Mont Maudit, one of the classical routes up Mont Blanc. Photograph by Pascal Tournaire

The mountain belongs to you only after you come down from it. Before that, you belong to the mountain. The most difficult part is always the descent, not the ascent. Too many mountaineers have failed to understand this, and have never made it back down. And when you have reached the peak . . . you are at your most vulnerable—all that needs to happen is for the weather to worsen a little, and you never return. You become inordinately tired, but you still have to come down. If the blizzard had caught you on your way up, you could always have turned back in the prime of your strength. The goal is the peak, but the victory is the return to the valley. Too often I read in books on mountaineering statements such as, "And with the last of their strength they reached the summit." Anyone who has ever climbed anything higher than a wooden ladder immediately asks how they made it back down. A number of times, I have made it to the summits of Himalayan peaks with a fair dose of surplus energy, and then I have been hit by a blizzard on the trip down. Then I was assaulted by the exhaustion caused by a long stay at high altitudes, and I have been afraid—I was on the point of letting go. I always explain to young climbers who face their first summit—as much effort as it takes to go up, it takes even more to come back down.

Hans Kammerlander

My passion for climbing is based on rope-climbing. The rope that links two climbers is the true symbol of classic mountaineering. Climbing on the same rope creates profound feelings of understanding, trust, friendship. Records don't mean that much without emotions of this sort, which any rope climber can experience, no matter what level of difficulty the climb.

Christophe Profit

In the course of my long career as a climber, I have lost a number of dear friends. All of them, like me, have accepted the risk factor as an integral part of their relationship with the mountains. None of them desired to die but, if they could have chosen, they would have chosen to leave this life while engaged in the activity they loved more than any other.

Pat Morrow

In athletic climbing, the risk has no importance—it is a matter of athletic performance. In mountaineering, the risk is the basic motivation, because what counts is not the pure difficulty, but the selection of the route by which you reach the top. The idea of conquest is the underlying concept of mountain climbing. If you set off knowing that there is no danger, you won't come back, because you'll be driving bolts anyway, then it makes no sense to speak of mountaineering. It is nothing but a climb in search of an easy success.

Heinz Mariacher

We who have the habit of climbing mountains know just how far superior to brute force is the will to persevere and attain a specific goal. We know that every height that is attained, every step that is taken is the product of patient and difficult efforts, and that desire is no substitute for action. A great many difficulties will arise, a great many obstacles will have to be overcome and avoided, but for us the will to do something is the ability to do it. Educated at this rough school, we return to our everyday occupations stronger and better prepared to face the obstacles along the road of life. We are made strong and serene by the memory of duties performed and victories won on other fields of battle.

Edward Whymper

Locked in the stretcher, I thought about our adventure that was about to end, and our unexpected victory. We always speak of the ideal as a goal toward which one strives without ever reaching it. For each of us, Annapurna is an ideal attained. For us, the mountain has always been a natural field of endeavor where, on the frontier between life and death, we have found the freedom that we were searching for with eyes tightly shut, as necessary for us as bread to the belly. The mountains gave us the gift of their beauty, and we adored them with the openness of children and revered them with the veneration that a monk has for the divine. Annapurna, toward which we ran with empty hands, is a treasure on which we will live as wealthy men for the rest of our lives. And with this awareness we turn the page—a new life begins. There are other Annapurnas in the lives of men.

Maurice Herzog

Introduction

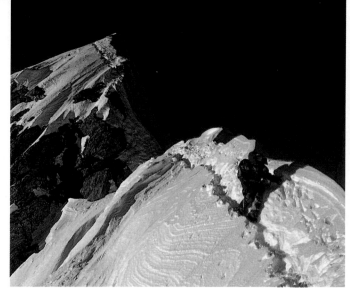

Vercors Massif, French Prèalps, the beginning of the summer of 1492 . . . In just one month and a half, Christopher Columbus would set sail from Palos on his epic voyage of discovery, and a group of "men at arms and men of the church" were setting out on a different sort of navigation. Instead of currents, waves, and the vast face of the ocean, they were challenging the sheer crags, the crumbling gullies, and the treacherous ledges of Mont Aiguille, called the "impervious mountain," a howling rock in the heart of the Dauphinè.

The equipment, techniques, and motivations of this expedition were as remote as could be from those of modern mountain climbers. Among the group, there was a maker of ladders and a stone cutter, specially summoned from the construction yards of the new cathedral of Montpellier. The order to climb the peak had been given by King Charles VIII. Three days after the peak had been scaled, a notary sent by the king to record the remarkable achievement certified that from the base of the mountain it was possible to see men moving about on the peak, and that the 6,880-foot summit had indeed been climbed.

The achievement did not go unacknowledged. François Rabelais, in his satirical epic, *Gargantua and Pantagruel*, wrote a few years later of "a mountain shaped like a gourd and which, to human memory, has never been climbed save by Doyac, a captain of artillery under King Charles VIII, who—with remarkable and ingenious devices—reached the summit, where he found an old ram." Doyac was, in reality, Antoine de Ville, lord of Dompjulien, mastermind and protagonist of the climb. The old ram was a flourishing herd of chamois, which had reached the top by climbing an intricate and perilous series of ledges. In 1991, shortly before modern mountain climbing celebrated its 500th anniversary, Reinhold Messner, probably the best known mountain climber of all time, was to return to Mont Aiguille via the original route pioneered by Antoine de Ville. Upon his return, he saluted de Ville as "the man who opened to humanity the gates to the vertical universe."

And yet, the fever of rocks, summits, and mountain adventure certainly did not begin with de Ville. For thousands of years, Europe feared the mountains. The Alps, the range that cuts the continent in two, were first climbed by fearful, bewildered men. During the Renaissance, the mountains were slowly rediscovered. Leonardo da Vinci and Albrecht Dürer depicted mountains in the backgrounds of their drawings and paintings; Josias Sim-

ler described the mountains in a treatise. Conrad Gesner climbed the Pilatus and other relatively easy Swiss peaks, while in 1573 Francesco de Marchi climbed a peak of the Gran Sasso in Italy, via "certain veins of rocks, a horrific place to traverse."

These were no more than isolated incidents, however. Mountain climbing became a fashionable enterprise in the Enlightenment and during the great voyages of geographic discovery. While Captain James Cook sailed the southern seas and ventured close to Antarctica, on a cold but beautiful evening, Michel-Gabriel Paccard and Jacques Balmat, subjects of the king of Sardinia, stood on the "Ceiling of Europe"—Mont Blanc. The following year, the feat was repeated by Horace-Bénédict de Saussure, the Genevan scholar and wealthy natural scientist who had egged the two climbers on in the first place. A few years later, the Emperor of Austria was to encourage the conquest of the Grossglockner, the highest mountain in the Hohe Tauern range. After Waterloo and the ensuing return of British travelers to Europe, the conquest of great mountains became systematic.

Only a few years passed before barometers and other scientific instruments—de rigueur in the first climbs up Mont Blanc—were left behind, and before British gentlemen (followed by French, German, Italian, and Swiss climbers) began to reach the great Alpine peaks, considering themselves to be athletes and adventurers, in the finest sense of the word. The ascent of Edward Whymper on the Matterhorn in 1865, and the tragedy that occurred during the climb down—claiming the lives of four of the seven men who first climbed "the most noble peak in Europe"—was the most celebrated indicator of the change. By this point, in the words of Sir Leslie Stephen (father of Virginia Woolf, who could boast of some exceptional climbs, especially in the Oberland), the Alps had become the "Playground of Europe."

By the end of the century, the sport had attained maturity. In 1881, Albert F. Mummery and his guide Alexander Burgener undertook a series of impressive climbs on the granite faces of Mont Blanc in an unfailingly pure mountaineering style. In 1887, Georg Winkler, an excellent solo climber, used a metal hook on the Vajolet Towers in the Dolomites, but the climbs he made were still extremely daunting. Shortly thereafter, Paul Preuss and Tita Piaz, Angelo Dibona and Hans Dülfer began to push to new heights the art of scaling the vertical and often brittle and crumbling walls of the Dolomites, crisscrossed with ledges. To the north, they

Below *Bill Makh reaches the peak of Mount Robson, the tallest mountain in the Canadian Rockies. Photograph by John Cleare*

Facing *Christophe Profit climbs the slopes on the south wall of Lhotse. Photograph by Pierre Béghin*

The first portion of the south wall of Lhotse is particularly hazardous because of the avalanches and rock falls. Attempting it by day would be suicidal. On the pillar, there are between 165 and 250 feet of very tough climbing, grades V and VI on crumbling rock. I got through that section wearing gloves, and every so often with the use of pitons. These sorts of obstacles at an altitude of 27,000 feet require enormous effort and are extremely tiring. I reached the peak at 2:20 on the afternoon of Tuesday, April 24, 1990. Then I tried to get down as fast as possible. I was scared. Even if there is not much snow, the avalanches up there can be triggered easily because the wall is so steep. I reached base camp at 8:00 the next morning.

Tomo Cesen

scaled the limestone walls sculpted by erosion of the Wilder Kaiser, the Karwendel, and other Tyrolian massifs.

Mountain climbing in the Himalayas and other great ranges of the world underwent an analogous development. At the turn of the century, the caravans of Prince Luigi Amedeo of Savoy-Aosta, the Duke of Abruzzi, and other forerunners of the great age to come were engaged in exploration and conquest rather than athletics. In 1939, however, K2 was almost climbed by Fritz Wiessner, a German climber from Dresden who had moved to America, a mountaineer of considerable talent and outstanding achievements. In the fifties, mountain climbers from all over the world—Britons and one famous New Zealander (Sir Edmund Hillary) on Everest and Kanchenjunga, Frenchmen on Annapurna and Makalu, Italians on K2, Austrians on Nanga Parbat and Dhaulagiri—continued the era of great achievements. In the Himalayas and the Karakoram, as in the Andes, the Hindu Kush, the Pamirs, New Zealand, and Alaska, the sport immediately took hold. Today, thousands of aficionados line up to climb the glaciers of Mont Blanc and Monte Rosa, the rock faces of the Sella Towers, ant the Campanile Basso of Brenta. And it is increasingly common for lines to develop on the southeast ridge of Everest, where Sir Edmund Hillary and Tenzing Norgay made their famed climb in 1953, on the West Buttress of Mount McKinley, and on many other great mountains, which have been transformed in a few years from myths to consumer attractions.

Is true mountaineering a thing of the past? Not at all. In its earliest days, skiing was strictly linked to the challenges of mountaineering, which developed with separate rituals, practitioners, and cultures; now skiing has invaded, radically modified, and, in some cases, ruined the Alps. And it is worth pointing out that, in the beginning, skiers were first and foremost mountaineers. During more or less the same years—the turn of the century or thereabouts—mountain excursions and hiking became an independent activity. The Austrian and German Alpenvereins were building trails as early as 1900, and today hundreds of thousands of people hike through the Dolomites around Mont Blanc and through the villages of Nepal. Many have climbed mountains, and many young climbers are tempted to progress to the mighty summits. No, mountain climbing is not dead. Even the last branch to spring from the tree—free-climbing, practiced at low altitudes—only at first took away from the ranks of mountaineering. Then, as the young athletes of

On October 17, 1986, Hans Kammerlander and I were making our way back to the base camp of Lhotse. I felt relaxed and serene. The next day, the era of "post-8,000," I felt light and liberated, because the whole world was open to me now. We all need a little bit of luck, because the mountains dwarf us so immensely. Mere humans can never "conquer" a mountain. "Lhagyelo," say the Tibetans, when they reach the top of a mountain or a high pass, and that is what I say too—"The Gods have triumphed." I am not proud of setting a record, because that is not how I think of it. I am not proud of the success that I sought with such determination. I am only proud of having survived.

Reinhold Messner

freeclimbing became more experienced and stronger, they returned to the high peaks. And the level of difficulty made a great leap forward on the Aiguilles of Chamonix and the Briançonnais, Mount Kenya, and the Towers of Trango.

Despite the development of competing sports, mountaineering, big wall- and cliff-climbing all constitute one of the great remaining adventures available to the city-dweller of today. From Milan, one can quickly reach Monte Rosa or Piz Badile; from Vienna or Munich one can drive to the Dolomites or the Wilder Kaiser; and Parisians can easily reach Mont Blanc and the Valais. Five hundred years after Antoine de Ville climbed in the Vercors Massif, and nearly a century after Preuss, climbing granite walls or snow ridges offers the same pleasure it always has. On the pages that follow, we present spectacular scenes on some of the most fabulous, forbidding, and beautiful mountains on Earth.

Considering the mysteries of the desire for conquest, Dino Buzzati, a great Italian author and journalist and himself a mountaineer, wrote the following about the conquest of Everest: "In the ancient castle, atop the proudest tower, there was a small room into which no one had ever gone . . . In that room had been stored poetry, with all the dreams, hopes, illusions, and beautiful useless things so necessary to life. Now where can we find it?" How can we answer this question? For every apprentice climber and every veteran mountaineer who climbs, there is still a little of the original poetry. One of the great virtues and one of the great mysteries of the mountains lies in this fact.

Finally, over the past few years, even mountain climbers have been working to limit the number of fixed ropes that are left, and ski lifts and roads that are built in the mountains. In the past, it is true, mountaineers have led the way for developers, road-builders, speculators, and resort operators. By protecting the Dolomites, Everest, K2, and Mont Blanc, we mountaineers are helping to preserve the great arenas for adventure on this planet, keeping them around for many generations yet to come.

The Himalayas and Karakoram
Peaks that Touch the Heavens

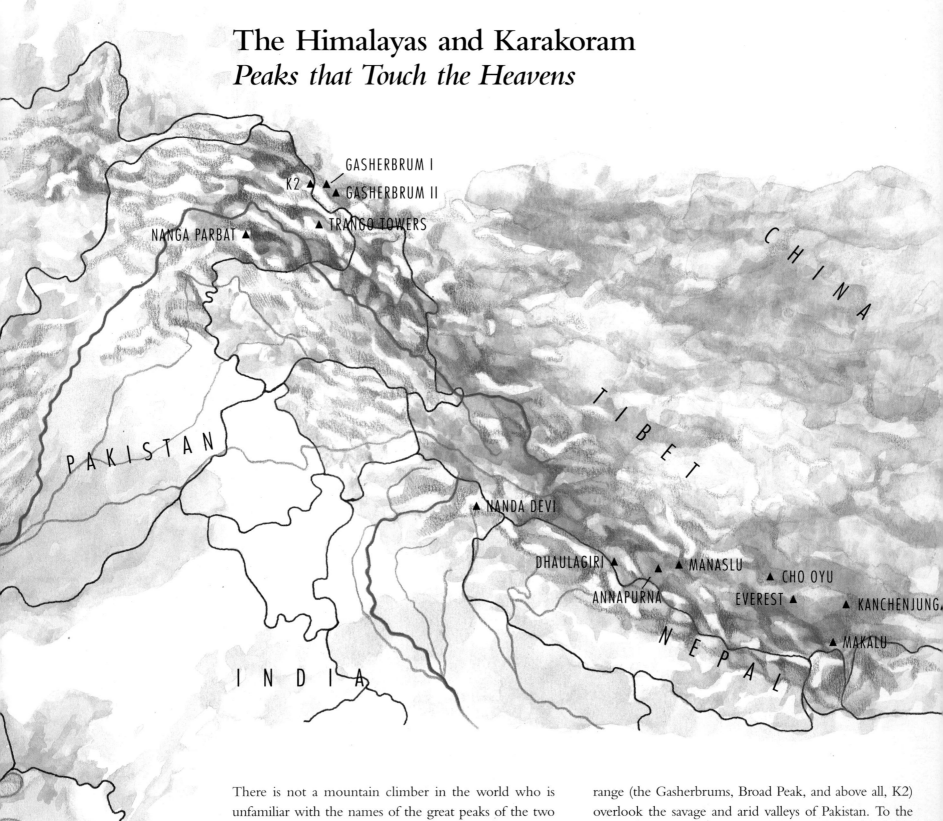

GASHERBRUM I
K2 ▲ ▲ GASHERBRUM II
▲ TRANGO TOWERS
NANGA PARBAT ▲

CHINA

TIBET

PAKISTAN

▲ NANDA DEVI

DHAULAGIRI ▲ ▲ MANASLU ▲ CHO OYU
ANNAPURNA EVEREST ▲ ▲ KANCHENJUNG.
▲ MAKALU

NEPAL

INDIA

There is not a mountain climber in the world who is unfamiliar with the names of the great peaks of the two great Asian ranges, the Himalayas and the Karakoram: the dark rocks of Everest, the icy arabesques of K2, the massive silhouettes of Kanchenjunga and Makalu, the sheer cliffs of Ama Dablam and Pumori, the gloomy moraines of the Baltoro Glacier, the vast expanses of the Tibetan highlands, the green valleys of Nepal. Many of the adventures that have taken place on these fabled peaks—those of George Leigh Mallory, Andrew Irvine, Sir Edmund Hillary and Tenzing Norgay, Achille Compagnoni, Lino Lacedelli, and Reinhold Messner—are well known even to those who have never been near a glacier.

The most astonishing fact about these ranges, however, is their sheer size. From the Indus in the west to the Brahmaputra in the east, the highest mountain range in the world extends for over 1,500 miles. There are fourteen peaks taller than 8,000 meters—roughly equivalent to 26,250 feet; over 100 top 7,000 meters—just under 23,000 feet.

The top 150 mountains in the world are all here. To the west, the 26,000-foot peaks of the Karakoram range (the Gasherbrums, Broad Peak, and above all, K2) overlook the savage and arid valleys of Pakistan. To the east, the mountains attain their greatest altitude with Mt. Everest. Facing Everest, and standing nearly as tall, are Lhotse ("South Mountain"), Kanchenjunga, Cho Oyu ("Goddess of the Turquoise"), and Makalu. Along this great mountain chain, there are other peaks that soar above the 8,000-meter mark—Annapurna, Dhaulagiri, Nanga Parbat, and Manaslu. Scattered among them are yet other savage giants, challenging, spectacular, and only slightly lower in altitude. It would be hard to imagine climbs more exciting than Shivling, Changabang, and Nanda Devi.

Today, the Himalayas and the Karakoram are in fashion. People stand in line to climb Everest, either trekking along the crowded trails, or on excursions that lead right up to the foot of the huge, sheer walls. Like a colossal wall, the Himalayas separate the environment, climate, and culture of Pakistan and India from the rest of central Asia. This is the meeting point of three of the world's great religions—Buddhism, Hinduism, and Islam. More than elsewhere, mountain climbers must consider themselves privileged guests, and act accordingly.

Everest
Mother of the Snows

29th of May, 1953... One step at a time, two men move carefully along a fragile ridge of snow separating Tibet and Nepal. Leaving behind them the rounded dome of the south peak, 28,710 feet above sea level, they cut off to the left, along the Nepalese side, over the giant ledges that soar straight up from the glacier of Kangshung. A sheer crevasse between the rock face and the ice allows them to scale a nearly vertical stretch. Then the ridge becomes a little less steep, a little wider. At exactly 11:30 that morning, five hours after setting out from the last camp, the two climbers have reached the highest point on earth: the peak of Everest, 29,028 feet above sea level. The honor of being the first men to tread the planet's "third pole" went to Edmund Hillary, a 34-year-old beekeeper from New Zealand, and Tenzing Norgay, a 37-year-old Nepalese Sherpa.

"Once Everest had been conquered, mountain climbing could begin in earnest," commented Eric Shipton, who first conceived the route along which Hillary and Tenzing actually climbed. In the years to follow; the members of the expedition (Hillary, Tenzing, and the team leader John Hunt) went from one speaking engagement to the next in an endless whirl of special events and galas. Tenzing was to become the "first Asian of humble birth in history to attain international fame and renown," in the words of Pete Boardman, one of the team that climbed the southwest face of Everest in 1975.

For Hillary and Tenzing, one doubt lingers. Were they truly the first to climb Everest? To find the answer, we must look far back in history It has been common knowledge for many years that the tallest mountain in the world stood at the border between Tibet and Nepal. The Tibetan lamas who drew the first map of the region on behalf of the Emperor in Beijing, between 1711 and 1717, showed, at the southern edge of the highlands, a mountain range 4,350 miles long. It was identified as the Choulu Lancma. A map published in 1733 in Paris by D'Anville shows the same mountains. In 1856, in an office in Calcutta, the final report of the Survey of India was drawn up, producing a map of the entire sub-continent. Peak XV, which is a summit visible on clear days all the way from the Plains of Bengal, was shown as standing 29,028 feet. The Nepalese called this giant *Sagarmatha*, while the Tibetans called it *Chomolungma*, "Mother Goddess of Harvests." The British prosaically named Peak XV after Sir George Everest, former director of the Survey.

Once the mountain was discovered, of course,

people began thinking about scaling it. As early as 1906, the English adventurers Bruce, Longstaff, and Mumm were planning an expedition, but the Tibetan and Nepalese borders were closed, and so all bets were off for several years. In 1920, permission was finally forthcoming-the administration in Lhasa granted the wish of the foreigners to "see the Chomolungma." The following year, the first expedition was on its way. After walking nearly 400 miles from Darjeeling to the Monastery of Rongbuk, nine Englislimen stood at the foot of the mountain. And a year later, the first serious effort to scale it took men above 8,000 meters-a yard under 26,250 feet-for the first time. "At 27,297 feet-we could make out the individual rocks on the summit," George Finch was to write. "But if we had kept climbing, we would never have got down alive." Two days after this effort, an avalanche killed a Sherpa.

Another attempt was made in 1924. On 4 June, E. E Norton made the climb alone, abandoning the line of the northeast ridge, continuing along a lengthy couloir and reaching an altitude of 28,123 feet before heading back down. Four days later, it was George Mallory and Andrew Irvine's turn to try At 12:50, they were seen following the line of the ridge. From afar, Noel Odell last saw them struggling up the Second Step, one of the major obstacles of the route above 28,000 feet. Then they disappeared, never to be seen again. Did they reach the peak? In 1980, Reinhold Messner wrote: "Their spirit is here; I feel that clearly. But I feel equally certain that they failed. I don't know how I know; but I know it." Finally, in 1999, an American expedition found the remains of George Leigh Mallory on a ledge a short distance from the crest. The climber's mummified body was at last given a decent burial, but there was still no trace of Andrew Irvine or the camera. Only that film could, thanks to some miracle of chemistry and freezing temperatures, tell us just how high the two climbers had reached.The tragic deaths led the 13th Dalai Lama to refuse any further requests to climb. Only in 1933 was a British team allowed to set off. Wyn Harris and L. K. Wager, and then Frank Smythe climbing solo, reached an approximate altitude of 27,880 feet. Attempts were made in 1935, 1936, and 1938, but fell short. After WW II changed the world's political geography, the Chinese occupation closed Tibet to foreigners, but Nepal opened its doors. In 1950, a group of British climbers caught their first glimpse of the colossal serac that seems to block the route up the south face. The fol-

The cold penetrated into my bones, but I was not concerned, because I could not feel it—I was blinded and bewitched by the magic of this remarkable place. During the climb, I saw enormous ice statues that were continually being reshaped, as if they were the fruit of a delirious creativity. The madness of the shapes, the play of the light, the length of the climb, the altitude, the silence—all these factors contributed to generating a state of exasperated emotion. This mineral universe was not, in fact, a dead world; it possessed a language that touched me profoundly. I was only a microbe on this giant being. I was hiking in the direction of the South Col, it was three in the morning, and I was at 24,300 feet. I don't know if it was the intensity of the scene that lay before my eyes or whether it was the dangerous effect of the altitude, but I began to shout; my joy exploded . . . Christine was puzzled, but she allowed me to take her picture, and that allowed her to catch her breath.

Pascal Tournaire

lowing year, Eric Shipton, who had been the head of the 1935 expedition, made the very difficult climb up the ridge of Pumori and observed the serac and, beyond it, the Western Cwm, the wall of ice of the Lhotse, the South Col. "That's the way up!" Shipton exclaimed in excitement. A few days later, together with Tom Bourdillon, Edmund Hillary, and Michael Ward, he followed that route all the way to the edge of the Cwm, an altitude of 20,669 feet.

The following year, to the consternation of the English, the government of Katmandu granted a Swiss expedition permission to climb. After crossing the Cwm and climbing the wall of the Lhotse, Raymond Lambert and Tenzing Norgay set out from a camp at the South Col in an effort to reach the summit. They made it to 28,200 feet before turning back.

"The time has come for the conquest," wrote John Hunt, the head of the new British expedition. He and the rest of the team suited their actions to these words. The group left London by steamer on February 12, 1952; on 10 March, a long line of porters left Katmandu and headed for the mountain. By the end of the month, they had set up the base camp. With considerable efficiency, the climbers made their way over the serac, the Cwm, and the steep ice wall of the Lhotse. On 21 May, Wilfrid Noyce and the Sherpa Annullu were on the South Col at an altitude of 26,181 feet. On 26 May, Bourdillon and George Evans reached the south peak, at 28,707 feet. There remained a "steep, narrow ridge that was anything but inviting." Hillary and Tenzing knew what to expect.

Forty years later, the ridge still poses problems. Technically, the ridge is not very difficult, but it is treacherous because of the enormous cornices that adorn it, and most of the nearly 400 climbers that have reached the top of Everest have had to make their way past it. In 1975, in heavy fog, Mick Burke fell to his death from that ridge; Burke was one of the best British climbers of all time. Sundare, a Sherpa, has climbed past it five times. In the forty years since Tenzing and Hillary first scaled Everest, the mountain has been climbed via thirteen separate routes; there is a guide to these routes, much like the guide to the Alps, entitled *Mount Everest*, written in German by the Polish author, J. Kielkowsky.

In good weather conditions and with the assistance of a team of Sherpas, even mountain climbers of

modest abilities have reached the top. A number of guides have organized collective expeditions to the peak. Cleanup expeditions have been made in order to clear debris from the South Col and the Nepalese and Tibetan base camps, and others are planned for the future. On the Khumbu side, a flood of thousands of trekkers reaches the base camp each year. On the Western Cwm, at an altitude of 21,000 feet, as many as a hundred people have set up camp at one time.

These are the kind of statistics one would expect from a classic mountain in the Alps. We should remember, however, that Everest remains the highest peak in the world, and those who climb it must contend with air so thin that there is only forty percent of the oxygen one breathes at sea level. Its walls and ridges are enormous and dangerous, exposed to the fury of the monsoons and the icy north winds. The two normal, relatively easy routes up are heavily traveled, but on the sheer walls of this colossus, great challenges remain and many tragedies continue. Even after its conquest, Everest—for the most part—is a mountain for exceptional climbers.

After the conquest by Hillary and Tenzing, the Swiss returned in 1956. Four climbers reached the

Above *A member of the French expedition of 1990 climbs the standard route up Everest, heading for Camp III.*

Facing *Christine Janin, the first woman to climb the highest peaks on all seven continents, poses at 28,000 feet, heading for the peak of Everest.*

Photographs by Pascal Tournier

summit. Luchsinger and Keiss scaled Lhotse, the southern subsidiary summit of Everest, but also the fourth-highest peak in the world, at 27,890 feet. In 1960, an Indian expedition attempted to scale the mountain from the south, while a Chinese team claimed to have reached the peak from the north, completing the route that had been blazed by Mallory and Irvine. In the West, the announcement met with skepticism; after another Chinese expedition in 1975, Dougal Haston, Doug Scott, and the rest of their team found a tripod and flag left behind by the Chinese at 29,028 feet. The third route to the peak was inaugurated in 1963. Tom Hombein and Willy Unsoeld made their way along this route up the gloomy and menacing west ridge.

In 1965, the Indians returned to the peak; from 1966 until 1969 Nepal closed its borders to mountain climbers. The border opened again the next year, and with that began the epic of the southwest face. Two international expeditions and one English expedition made the attempt, without success. Then, in 1975, Chris Bonington and his team conquered this route. A detour to the left enabled the party to avoid the band of rocks that had stymied earlier attempts. Along the difficult gully that proved to be the key to success on this route, Nick Escourt and Paul "Tut" Braithwaite were pushed to the limit. And then the way was clear. On 26 September, Dougal Haston and Doug Scott continued along steep snowfields interrupted repeatedly by difficult walls of rock. They reached the south peak in the late afternoon.

Technically, the route had been completed. What were they to do? "On the Alps, it is legitimate to climb a route without reaching the peak, but things are different in the Himalayas. We knew that we had not yet reached our goal," Haston wrote later. And so the two climbers continued. On the ridge, conditions were better than they had been on the wall; once again Haston was the first to climb the last vertical stretch. They both reached the peak, where they discovered the Chinese tripod and banner, took photographs, and surveyed the view They returned to the south peak and bivouacked under extremely harsh conditions. As they descended the next day, they encountered the second team on its way up. Pete Boardman and Pertemba reached the peak amid worsening weather. But Mick Burke, without a rope, disappeared on the ridge. He may well have reached the peak before falling to his death.

In the years that fallowed, there was a steady alternation of great conquests and great tragedies. In 1974, the French climber Gerard Devoassuoux and four Sherpas were killed in an avalanche. In 1978, Reinhold Messner and Peter Habeler reached the peak without oxygen. Two years later, Messner reached the peak again, this time alone, without oxygen, along the more traditional route, from Tibet. And it was from Ti-

bet, which had finally been opened once again to foreign climbers, that the most interesting pages of history come down to us. An American team attempted the huge east face of the Kangshung glacier in 1981, and then tried again in 1983; three climbers reached the peak. The year before, in 1982, an English expedition attempted the northeast ridge; tragically, Pete Boardman and Joe Tasker, certainly one of the finest teams of Himalayan climbers ever, lost their lives in this effort.

In 1984, an Australian team conquered the Great Couloir of the North Face; in 1988, a group of Chinese, Japanese, and Nepalese climbers broadcast the first live television pictures from the peak. A light expedition headed by Steve Venables opened a route on the east slope. In 1990, just a few miles from the new eastern route, the Slovenian climber Tomo Cesen scaled the south wall of Lhotse, where just a few months previous the Polish climber Jerry Kukuczka died. This is the most daunting wall in the Himalayas, and it forms part of the Everest group. In 1991, the Italians Fausto De Stefani and Giuliano De Marchi came down from the north wall of Everest with serious frostbite. A few days later, Battista Bonali completed the new route that De Stefani and De Marchi had been attempting.

World-wide notoriety came however to the normal Nepalese Everest route in the pre-monsoon season of 1996. A violent storm which struck the mountain was responsible for the death of nine climbers between the 10th and 12th of May. Most of the victims were clients of the commercial expeditions led by the New Zealander Rob Hall and the American Scott Fischer, two guides who also lost their lives in the blizzard.

At once accessible and treacherous, inviting and vengeful, Everest is still there. Topographical measurements actually show that the mountain has grown since it was first measured in the nineteenth century, by a good hundred to a hundred thirty feet. If we want to understand how much effort this "accessible" mountain requires, however, let us listen to the words of Reinhold Messner, describing his solo expedition of 1980. "During my solo climb, I was careful to avoid risks. And yet on my first day. . . I fell twenty-six feet down a crevasse, and came close to dying. . . Only when I had returned to the foot of the mountain, when all of the dangers and tribulations were behind me, when I was sure that I could no longer fall, could no longer die by asphyxiation or freeze to death, only then did I collapse."

Left *Everest's difficult northeast ridge, shown here, is where the famous English climbers Pete Broadman and Joe Tasker disappeared in 1982. Photograph by Chris Bonington*

Facing *Mick Burke climbs up to Camp VI on the southwest wall during the English expedition of 1975. Photograph by Chris Bonington*

PAGES 36–37
Two members of the first Canadian expedition to climb Everest celebrate on the peak in 1982. Photograph by Pat Morrow/First Light

Another step, and the northeast ridge was hidden by a curl of snow. This was where Pete Boardman had last seen Mick Burke in 1975. He and Pertemba were on their way down; Mick was going for the summit on his own. He never came back. My head was filled with thoughts of lost friends, of Nick Estcourt who forced the Everest Rock Band and died on K2, of Dougal Haston who went to the summit of Everest with Doug Scott, and died skiing near his home in Switzerland.

And then suddenly I was there. Odd, Bjørn, and Pertemba were beckoning to me, shouting, their voices muffled by their oxygen masks. I crouched in a fetal position and just cried and cried in great gasping sobs— tears of exhaustion, tears of sorrow for so many friends, and yet tears of fulfillment for something I had so much needed to do and had done with people who had come to mean a great deal to me. I had at last reached the summit of Everest.

Chris Bonington

I've been lucky, or cursed, depending how you look at it, in trying to climb Mount Everest by its two easiest routes, from both the north and south sides. In 1982, I dodged falling ice blocks and one major avalanche while on my way to the summit via the South Col route with the first Canadian Everest Expedition. With four team members killed and half our team leaving for home before the expedition was finished, the crippling psychological aspect of proceeding higher on the mountain was a major factor. I was weakened by the overall experience and threatened by the unknown, for this was my first time at altitudes over 8,000 meters.

The psychological barrier was broken down for me by my teammate Laurie Skreslet, who made the summit two days before I did. When he flashed his victorious grin to me back at Camp II, he said I should have been with him with my camera to photograph the sunrise over Tibet. He left Camp IV at the South Col early in the morning and was high on the summit ridge when the first rays of light crept across the Tibetan Plateau. Inspired by the image he painted with his words, I did manage to take photos from the same vantage point. As a dedicated adventure photographer, I was driven to the top in order to take photographs, and the climbing experience was only secondary.

For many, Everest is a love/hate relationship. I've met climbers who have returned two or more times to climb Everest, and the sparkle never seems to leave their eyes. In 1991, I chatted under a canopy of Buddhist prayer flags near Mallory base camp with Ang Rita, the Sherpa who has made it to the top seven times. Without oxygen. For him, it is a way to make a living. However, he seemed to enjoy his notoriety and liked the idea that he had been to the top of that mountain five times more than Reinhold Messner.

Pat Morrow

This photograph was taken on the third day, just over Camp II, on the occasion of our last attempt to climb to the summit of Everest via the long and difficult west ridge. In the six weeks prior to this, we had installed fixed ropes and had set up the first two camps. From Camp II, at 22,310 feet, we wanted to continue climbing in Alpine style. There were still four of us when, early in the morning, we began to make our way up through the fresh snow above the camp. Taking pictures at high altitude requires a great deal of discipline. One must necessarily be very precise. In order to take these pictures, I had to remove three pairs of gloves, I had to change the lens, and then I had to kneel in the deep snow while wearing a backpack weighing more than thirty-five pounds. At almost 23,000 feet, that is truly tiring. The camera must always be easily available. That seems easy enough, but the temptation to stow the camera away in the backpack—so as to have it out of the way—is very tough to resist. And once your camera is in your backpack, that is exactly where it stays.

Robert Bösch

Below *A member of the Australian expedition up Everest in 1984 climbs to the North Col from the west; in the background can be seen Lho La, Pumori, and Cho Oyu, one of the lesser known "8,000s."*

Facing *A team ascends the north wall of Everest.*

Photographs by Colin Monteath/Hedgehog House

There were just 3,000 feet left to climb, and it did not seem insurmountable. I was in good shape, and I decided to set out alone, at 8:30 A.M. The tracks I left in the snow were erased rapidly by the wind. There was crusted snow, and progress was tiring. In that infernal setting, however, I rediscovered the sensation of hyperemotion, typical of high altitudes. I concentrated, willing myself not to succumb. It was pleasurable, a sort of intoxication and a sense of completeness, but at the same time there was something terrible about it. My heart was racing, I felt like crying, I worked hard not to give in. I had to get a grip on myself if I was going to go on. I found myself with Christine at nearly 28,000 feet. We had to reach the south summit before nightfall. On the south summit, I saw the final ridge; it was magnificent and seemed close at hand. I waited for Christine, and then we started up the ridge. It was hard for us to realize that this last hundred yards or so was the culmination of a long countdown. We were actually at the top of the tallest mountain on earth. With the last rays of sun, Nepal embraced us. To the east, the shadow of Everest extended to the edge of an ocean of clouds over Tibet, while Makalu and Lhotse, golden sentinels, emerged from the sunset.

Pascal Tournaire

Annapurna
The Savage Mountain

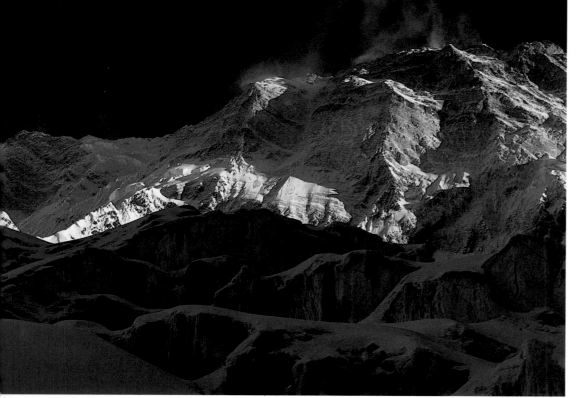

Above, upper *At an altitude of about 18,000 feet, a team prepares to climb the ridge of Fang, a satellite of Annapurna often visited by lightweight expeditions. Photograph by Marco Majrani*

Above, lower *The south wall of Annapurna glitters in the light of dawn. Photograph by Pascal Tournaire*

Facing *Ian Clough climbs up the steepest stretch of the south wall in 1970. Photograph by Chris Bonington*

The dawns of Pokhara are certainly among the world's most beautiful. While the surrounding plains, the small town, and the lake still slumber in shadow, the huge mountains are golden with the first rays of the sun. In the distance to the east is Manaslu, 26,781 feet tall, solitary, and difficult. It has recently become quite fashionable among climbers. To the west is the brilliant white pyramid of Dhaulagiri, 26,811 feet in height. This mountain, which has no easy access route, has indicated the way along the Kali Gandaki to Hindu pilgrims and Dolpo traders for thousands of years.

Annapurna, however, at 26,504 feet, dominates the view. Its south wall is nearly four miles wide and more than a mile high. For the locals, Annapurna is "She Who is Full of Food," that is, the goddess of harvests. Above all, Annapurna is a mountain with a long and impressive history. The first chapter in this history began on the afternoon of June 14, 1950, just a few months after Nepal opened its borders to foreigners. That day, two French climbers, Maurice Herzog and Louis Lachenal, reached the peak of the first 8,000-meter mountain to be climbed by a human being. Herzog was delighted, but Lachenal just wanted to get off the mountain. When Herzog dropped his gloves, and the two climbers watched them skid down the steep slope and then drop off into the empty space of a crevasse, the tone had been set for the dramatic hours to follow. The descent was a harrowing ordeal, and had it not been for the tough-minded determination of Lionel Terray and Gaston Rébuffat—two of the finest French mountain climbers ever—the mountain's conquerors would never have made it back to base camp and, in the end, back to France. They suffered serious frostbite, however. Lachenal took a serious fall near Camp V, which was a nightmarish bivouac in a crevasse rocked by avalanches. The team doctor, Jacques Oudot, was forced to perform amputations on the climbers without anesthesia. All of these alarming events are described in Herzog's book, *Annapurna, Premier 8,000.*

The second chapter in Annapurna's history came twenty years later. In late March 1970, a small British expedition led by Chris Bonington reached the "Sanctuary," a rim-shaped valley at the foot of the south face. The path they followed was to become one of the best known trekking routes in the world; along it, just a few days earlier, Don Whillans encountered what seemed to him to be a Yeti. As the climber later wrote, "One of those dark spots seemed to move . . . I could just

Climbing on Gasherbrum I, Annapurna, Makalu, and Lhotse I found, partially covered in snow, the bodies or the skeletons of many climbers who had been captured by the mountains that they had challenged. At times, I buried them as best I was able, in a crevasse or in the snow. At times, I walked past them in silence, unable to perform any act of piety for them.

Hans Kammerlander

glimpse a leaping motion . . . the thing was moving on all fours, making very fast leaps . . . I took a photo of one of the prints, and you could see scrapes in the snow that looked like the marks of claws." Two months later, on May 27, 1970, Whillans and his companion Dougal Haston were dealing with a different cause for excitement. After two months of working their way up gullies exposed to avalanches, across razor-sharp ice ridges, of climbing difficult rocks well above the 7,000-meter level, the two of them finally were standing on the snowy peak of the mountain. It was another remarkable undertaking, successfully completed by a light expedition just like the 1950 climb to the peak.

This climb up the south wall opened a chapter in the history of world mountain climbing of remarkable ascents of 8,000-meter (about 26,250 feet) peaks by way of the steepest, tallest, and most difficult walls: the southeast and east walls of Everest, and the west wall of Makalu. Over a thousand miles away, the Messner brothers climbed Nanga Parbat along the Rupal Face, completing yet another page of the chapter that was being written.

The rest of the history of Annapurna is more commonplace, and yet rife with drama all the same. In 1973, on the north slope, four Japanese climbers, a Sherpa, and the Italian climbers Leo Cerruti and Miller Rava died in a colossal avalanche that buried an entire camp. In 1981, a Polish group which included Jerzy Kukuczka opened a new route up the south face. Another route was opened by two very young Catalonian climbers many years later. In 1985, Hans Kammerlander and Reinhold Messner conquered the daunting northwest face under an incessant rain of avalanches. During a second attempt, Reinhard Patscheider fell over 1,300 feet and miraculously survived. In October 1992, Pierre Béghin, France's finest climber, died on the terrible south face.

"Luck is the gift of the gods, but the requirements for success—dedication and strength—are something that only we ourselves can create," wrote Reinhold Messner on his return, after conquering his eleventh 8,000-meter peak. With these words Maurice Herzog ended his book: "Annapurna is a treasure that we will have for all the rest of our lives . . . there are other Annapurnas in the lives of human beings." The challenge of the great white mountain remains.

Night at Camp IV was awful. The rage of the tempest forced us to brace the tent from within in order to keep it from flying away with us inside. We were seated inside the plastic igloo, our arms stretched upwards and hands jammed into the air vents of the side walls. Once the icy chill began to penetrate into our gloves, we had to stop that. The fury of the blizzard was buffeting our tent with such violence that the noises sounded like guns going off. Above us, the storm was tearing away, block by block, the protective wall that we had built. At 4:30 A.M., we decided to set off for the peak. "There are no more thoughts," whispered Messner. "Our thoughts turn into will . . . All that remains is the will to continue, to complete this climb because the summit is there . . ."

Hans Kammerlander

Nanga Parbat
Devourer of Men

August 1895 . . . Accompanied by two Gurkhas, the English climber Albert Frederick Mummery climbed up the valleys at the foot of Nanga Parbat, the 8,000-meter peak closest to the Indian lowlands. The small team made their way up the valley of Rupal. They shifted over to the valley of Diamir, and then Mummery disappeared at an altitude of just over 6,000 meters, or close to 20,000 feet. He holds the honor of being the first illustrious European victim of the Himalayas.

Summer 1934 . . . A German expedition led by Willi Merkl climbed to an altitude of 25,590 feet on Nanga Parbat. The team was hit by a raging storm, and four climbers died, among them Merkl himself and the remarkably skilled glacier climber Willo Welzembach. Three years later, a massive avalanche at Camp IV buried all seven of the climbers and all nine of the high-altitude bearers of a German expedition. Nanga Parbat began to acquire a reputation as the "cursed mountain."

Then came July 3, 1953, when Hermann Buhl, a young climber from Austria, made his way alone up the last snow ridge that led to the peak at 26,658 feet. It was a remarkable achievement, close to impossible, and it was destined to go down in history. The Austrian climbed the last 4,300 feet all alone. And on June 27, 1970, the brothers Gunther and Reinhold Messner reached the top of the Rupal Face, the tallest and most challenging on the mountain. Fatigue and their scanty equipment (they did not even have a rope!) kept them from descending the way they had come up. They went down the Diamir face. After two atrocious bivouacs, by now almost at the foot of the most difficult part, Gunther Messner disappeared under a massive avalanche. Reinhold survived and looked for his brother for a day and the following night; then he was forced to set off. Reinhold's life was saved by some passing mountaineers, with whose help he made his way to the bottom of the mountain in a series of adventures. In the autumn, most of his toes were amputated.

Among the highest mountains on the planet, Nanga Parbat is certainly the one with the most frequent tales of danger and loss of life. It is also the mountain closest to the lowlands, and this explains the great number of expeditions that attempt it (over twenty a year since 1985) and also partially explains the dangers. Directly exposed to the brunt of the monsoons, Nanga Parbat often flails climbers with sudden raging gales and shifting snow. Aside from Mummery, its most illustrious climbers have almost always been Germanic.

Left, upper Barry Blanchard climbs the Rupal Face on Nanga Parbat at an altitude of 22,638 feet. Photograph by Marc F. Twight / Agence Freestyle

Left, lower The American climbers Barry Blanchard and Ward Robinson are forced by bad weather to retreat from the Rupal Face; this was the seventh day of climbing on the August 1988 expedition. Photograph by Marc F. Twight / Agence Freestyle

Facing The daunting Rupal Face on Nanga Parbat is one of the most difficult and dangerous in the Himalayas. Photograph by Marc F. Twight / Agence Freestyle

PAGES 50–51
Barry Blanchard, Ward Robinson, and Kevin Doyle, hampered by a storm, rappel down the highest part of the Rupal Face. Photograph by Marc F. Twight / Agence Freestyle

After only five days of climbing on the Rupal Face of Nanga Parbat, we found ourselves at 7,850 meters (25,755 feet) in a storm.

It was suicide to stay put and wait it out because we had food for only two more days. It was suicidal to rappel back into the Merkl Gully because all of the avalanches funnelled into the couloir and increased in both speed and violence as the deep gully concentrated them. The choice was easy; we all preferred to die trying to get down rather than to die starving. The mountain had already killed fifty-three people during numerous attempts to climb it—for me Nanga Parbat is the world's largest tombstone.

Halfway down the gully the four of us were swept away by an avalanche. We all hung on a single ice screw as tons of snow pummeled us breathless in the sickening atmosphere of defeat. Unable to unweight the screw, we thrashed wildly, struggling to hang onto life, with our heads facing down, creating air pockets to breathe in. It went on and on. The ice screw held. The avalanches let up. After four more rappels we reached relative sanctuary. But in the confusion of darkness, exhausted from climbing continually for fifteen hours, Barry (Blanchard) and Kevin (Doyle) lost our only two ropes and I dropped one of the tents. With 3,000 meters (9,842 feet) between us and base camp, the future was fairly bleak.

At dawn we began downclimbing without too much hope of making it. The storm raged on. At 6,900 meters (22,638 feet) we discovered a sun-bleached pack clipped into some pitons at an old belay station. Barry knifed it open and found two fifty-meter ropes, sixty pitons, twelve ice screws, a stove, and some chocolate bars. In 1984, four Japanese climbers had disappeared in the Merkl Gully, and before abandoning the mountain, their compatriots left them this gift in case they managed to return. A day and a half later we reached base camp.

Marc F. Twight

The four expeditions described were the most important, the most dramatic, and the best known. We should add to the list the expedition of 1932, in which the route to the Silberplateau was discovered, providing access to the highland that is crucial in any climb to the peak. Another noteworthy expedition went up in 1939, and its members—among them Heinrich Harrer, the first to climb the north face of the Eiger—ended their climb in a British prisoner-of-war camp, because World War II had broken out during the ascent. In 1962, another German expedition made the second successful climb to the peak and opened the route that is now the most commonly used. On the way down, Sigi Löw died. Another route that has been used more than once was discovered and first climbed in 1976 by the Austrian climber Hans Schell and his team. Two years later, on the great wall of Diamir, Reinhold Messner opened a new route, solo. Messner had already made two unsuccessful attempts, in 1973 and 1977, and he had experienced endless hours of fear at the base camp.

Messner placed his reliance on years of experience and a remarkable inner strength; he began his way back up the mountain from the exact spot where an avalanche had killed his brother and narrowly missed him nearly a decade earlier, and he continued upward despite another huge avalanche, triggered by an earthquake. On August 9, 1978, at 26,658 feet, he became the first man to climb one of the fourteen tallest mountains in the world entirely on his own. "I felt that I was a shadow . . . only action can serve as a response to the essential questions in life . . . I myself was the answer, and the questions no longer had any meaning." This is how Reinhold Messner's diary described his feelings upon reaching the peak. The descent, amidst heavy snowfall and fog, was an only slightly less difficult undertaking.

The dramatic history of Nanga Parbat continues. In 1982, the Swiss climber Hermann Bühler successfully ascended the southeast face. Later, Polish climbers made other noteworthy ascents and, in 1990, the South-Tirolean Hans Kammerlander was the first to ski down from the peak; upon his return, he wrote of a dangerous descent on a treacherous route over unstable snow.

The mountain drew me on with a magical force. I encountered it for the first time in 1968. I was young, a restless and fiery spirit, and I simply wanted to climb up this mountain of my dreams. A number of major avalanches and an accident involving a fellow climber had forced us to stop. And that did nothing more than to heighten my desire to reach the peak. In 1985, after climbing four more 8,000-meter peaks, I attempted to climb the Diamir Face, and I climbed this giant slope twice. Nanga Parbat stopped me once again with a rock fall. Great snow falls made me sense the cold and fatal breath of imminent avalanches. The dream never abandoned me. I truly reached the summit in 1988. It was the payback for a courtship that had lasted twenty years, twenty years of waiting, hoping, and facing disappointment. But it was not over, not even after a wonderful hour at the summit. I barely managed to survive a rock avalanche in a narrow gully during the descent.

Sigi Hupfauer

Below and right *Climbers from a German expedition scale Nanga Parbat during a 1988 attempt. Photographs by Sigi Hupfauer*

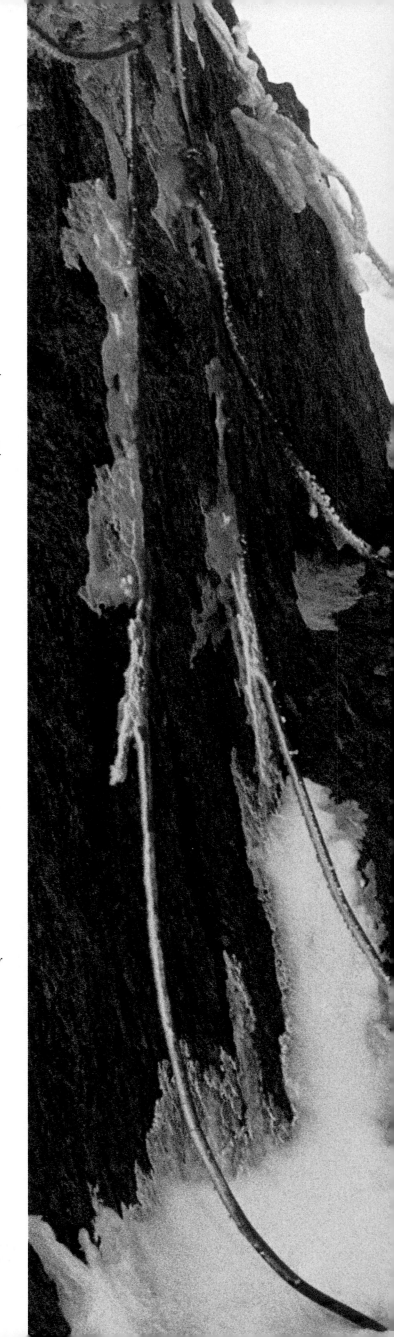

Above and right *Members of the 1985 German expedition attempt the difficult ascent of Nanga Parbat in particularly harsh conditions. Photographs by Michl Dacher*

Frost covered the inner lining of the tent, hanging down grimly over my face. In my partially wakened state, I executed precise and pre-planned climbing movements, and suddenly I was alone. It was still night, and I could see the stars through the icy canvas of the tent. A great deal of time passed before I managed to relax. Although I could not understand the cause of my panic, I continued to be afraid. I was afraid of being here, afraid of continuing, afraid of being a man. It wasn't the fear of falling that was paralyzing me; it was as if I was lost in this being alone. At 5 A.M., at the first light, I made my final decision: "I am descending and going home." I curled up in my sleeping bag and fell back to sleep. But the peace in my heart did not last long. From time to time I would see the rock pillar towering above me, the Diamir Face of Nanga Parbat. Perhaps I should try once more. "The Nanga, solo," I thought to myself. What is this? I have decided to climb down, and I'm thinking of climbing up!

Reinhold Messner

K2
The Great Pyramid

Above *Rick Ridgeway, one of the members of the American expedition on K2 in 1978, sets off from Camp III along the northeast wall. Photograph by John Roskelley*

Facing *Ridgeway, wearing a metal mask to protect his face from the harsh sunlight, heads for Camp V along a razor's edge ridge. He still has to make the dangerous traverse across Abruzzi Ridge and the final climb to the summit. Photograph by John Roskelley*

It was six in the evening on July 31, 1954, when, in the sky over the Karakoram, on the border between Pakistan and China, two men wrote their names on one of the most celebrated pages in the history of expedition climbing. Lino Lacedelli, 29, from Cortina d'Ampezzo in the Italian Dolomites, was a virtuoso climber. Achille Compagnoni, 40, born in Santa Caterina Valfurva, at the foot of the Cevedale and the Gran Zebrù, was accustomed to the rough climbing techniques of the central and western Alps. At 28,253 feet that evening, the two souls of Italian mountain climbing came together.

"It seemed to rise straight up like a perfect cone, unbelievably tall. I was speechless." With these words, sixty-six years before Compagnoni and Lacedelli made their climb, another first-class adventurer described the K2. Sir Francis Younghusband, at the time a captain in Her Majesty's dragoons, was the first westerner to see the great mountain from up close, the first to travel around it and to admire its remarkable symmetry—four ridges, four faces, and at the top an unattainable and perfect icecap. The year was 1888, and Younghusband was traveling and seeking adventure across Asia. Later, he was to take part in the march to relieve the besieged garrison of Chitral, and he was a member of the first expedition to Everest in 1921. In 1888, he was the first to witness something that is well known today. Everest is colossal, Makalu boasts astonishing rock walls, and Kanchenjunga defends itself with terrifying ice cliffs. But K2 is the most impressive of them all, the most difficult, the most dangerous of the "tall 8,000s," the four mountains on earth that are over 8,500 meters tall.

K2 was sighted and named by an English surveyor named T. G. Montgomerie in 1856. Five years later, the Godwin Austen expedition observed it from the Baltoro Glacier. Immediately afterward, some of the great mountain climbers of the time came to have a try at K2. K2 is enormous even in comparison to its neighbors—the six peaks of the Gasherbrum ("Mountains of Light" for the local inhabitants, the Balti), Masherbrum ("Wall of Snow"), the Muztagh Tower, and Broad Peak.

The first attempt was made in 1892. A trio of climbers—the Englishman William Conway, the Austrian Oskar Eckenstein (inventor of modern crampons), and the Swiss guide Matthias Zurbriggern—made a half-hearted try at climbing K2, and then went on to climb to 22,900 feet on the nearby Golden Throne, setting a world record for the time. Ten years later, Eckenstein came back, together with the Irish climber Alastair

As eighty-kilometer (50 miles per hour) winds whipped over the summit of K2 and the temperature plunged to minus 20°C (4° below zero Fahrenheit), we feared Wickwire would not survive the night. Early the next morning, Ridgeway and I climbed toward the summit to find our teammate and help him down. Suddenly, out of the whipping blasts of wind-blown snow, Wickwire appeared traversing toward us, hypothermic and frostbitten, but still alive and able to descend. We offered our assistance, but he urged us to continue to the top. Not having a rope to help him, Ridgeway and I wished him well, and set a steady pace to the summit. At two o'clock, under cloudless skies, with no wind, and a view that stretched into three countries, we stood on top having climbed the second highest mountain without bottled oxygen. More than twenty-five years since the first American attempt, K2, the "American" mountain, finally felt our footsteps.

John Roskelley

Facing *Steve Swenson, member of the U.S. expedition of 1990, makes his way around a snow cornice at 22,638 feet on the south wall of K2.*

Right *Greg Mortimer, another member of the expedition, climbs the slopes above Camp II at an altitude of 24,000 feet.*

Photographs by Greg Child

When I was thirteen years old, I read the book that changed my life. It was the story of the first ascent of K2 by the Italian mountaineers Compagnoni and Lacedelli. That story of adventure inspired me to become a climber, and K2 became the candle I hovered around, like a moth, for many years as I tried to climb it.

I first saw K2 in 1983, from the slopes of Broad Peak. Though Broad Peak is high, K2 rises far above it, The sight of that jagged black tooth with clouds streaming from its summit filled me with fear and fascination. Four years later, I finally set foot on K2, with two Americans. We were ambitious, as all young and foolish men should be, and we dreamed of a new route climbed in Alpine style. We inspected the east face, but it was a terrible wall of seracs that sent avalanches down all day. Then we attempted the Abruzzi Ridge of the first ascent; no luck. We then tried the south face, reaching 7,100 meters (23,294 feet) before a storm mercifully forced us down. We tried, we lost, and we promised to return. And we did. In 1990, I finally stood on the summit of K2.

Greg Child

Crowley and the Austrian Hans Pfannl. Then it was the Italians' turn. In 1909, Luigi Amedeo di Savoia, the Duke of the Abruzzi, began his succession of ascents and descents on the Baltoro Glacier. With the royal mountain climber were seven guides from Courmayeur, the photographer Vittorio Sella, and a number of assorted assistants. This was the same group that first scaled Ruwenzori, Mount Saint Elias, and a number of peaks in the Caucasus range. On K2, the duke found the best way up—the long and jagged ridge that climbs on the southwest side to the great snow shoulder at 23,620 feet. The duke and his fellow climbers did not get very far up, but ever since then the route to the top of K2 is called the Abruzzi Spur.

In 1928, an Italian geographical expedition surveyed K2. In 1938, the American climber Charles Houston made a serious attempt and reached 21,490 feet. The year after that, Fritz Wiessner, a German who emigrated from his native Dresden to the United States and who had made some spectacular climbs in the Dolomites, made an attempt. On the evening of June 19, climbing on rocks at an altitude of 27,558 feet, Wiessner came heartbreakingly close to a triumph that would have gone down in the history of mountain climbing. The piercing cold and the fears of the Sherpa Pasang Lama forced him to descend. Then the expedition was hit by tragedy, with the deaths of three high-altitude porters and the American climber Dudley Wolfe. In 1953, Houston tried again, but was unsuccessful.

In 1954, the Italian expedition led by Ardito Desio made its attempt and was crowned with success. The passage of time and the difficulties the climbers were facing molded a national consensus of support for the expedition leader and his team. One climber, Mario Puchoz, a guide from Courmayeur, died from massive internal bleeding. The evening before the final climb, Walter Bonatti, a major figure in Alpine mountain climbing, narrowly escaped death, together with his high-altitude porter, in a nightmarish freezing camp at 25,590 feet. Then, at last, they reached the peak.

From 1960 until 1975, tensions between Pakistan, India, and China banished all foreigners from the Baltoro region of the Karakoram. When the ban was lifted, the procession of great climbers began once again. In 1977, a Japanese team scaled the west ridge. In 1979, Reinhold Messner and his redoubtable international team failed to reach the top along the "Magic Line" from the southwest; they did, however, make the peak following the route used in 1954. In 1983 and 1984, a Japanese expedition and another Italian expedition climbed K2 from the north, setting out from the deserts of Chinese Turkistan. In 1986, twenty-seven climbers reached the peak. Among them was the young French phenomenon, Benoît Chamoux, who climbed from 16,400 feet to the peak and returned in just twenty-four hours!

There were tragedies as well as victories, though. K2 is an unforgiving place, battered by furious storms, falling rocks, and avalanches, and is subject to radical changes in weather. K2 kills. Elsewhere in the Himalayas, inexpert climbers die fairly often. On K2 even the best climbers die. In 1978, the English climber Nick Escourt lost his life. Among the thirteen climbers who lost their lives during the "black summer" of 1986 were famous climbers like the Englishman Alan Rouse, the Italian Renato Casarotto, and the Pole Woyciech Wroz.

Then came a hiatus during which "Free K2," an expedition organized in 1990 by the preservation association Mountain Wilderness, reminded mountain climbers of the world just how much damage an expedition can do to a Himalayan peak. The expedition returned from the Abruzzi Spur and from the moraines of the Baltoro Glacier carrying miles of rope and tons of scrap metal left by previous climbers. Columns of dreary and rank-smelling black smoke rose from bonfires near the base camp.

In 1991, the mountain climbers returned in style. Two world-class French climbers, Christophe Profit and Pierre Béghin made an attempt to conquer the northwest ridge. This route had been tried, unsuccessfully, by many previous expeditions. Profit was the champion of "lightning climbs" and of "enchaînements" on Mont Blanc, while Béghin was a seasoned veteran of the Himalayas. It took them forty-five days of trying and nights of hell in mountain gales, inching across terribly dangerous, avalanche-ridden slopes, before they finally reached the peak, once again at sunset. It was 6:50 in the evening when Christophe and Pierre hugged each other and took a photograph of themselves at 28,253 feet. Night was falling rapidly, and the climb down was terrifying. "We are just tiny things up there," were Profit's words upon descending.

When I recall the days to the summit, it is like recalling a dream. I remember the coughing of my friends in our tents, and their mumbling dreams at night, as if they were possessed by spirits. And I remember the sound of the stove puttering pathetically against the morning cold, as if the flame had rigor mortis. The look of a man at 8,000 meters is sad, for you eat like a sparrow and waste away into a skeleton, as

if evaporating into the ether. More than anything, I recall the morning cold that froze the vapor in my nostrils into plugs, that sapped the blood in my hands, and that tasted like blue metal.

Higher up, the world became stranger. The squeak of my axes and crampons in the snow became sentences spoken by imaginary persons. Every step was a battle of willpower as we climbed at

the cruising altitude of a jet. On the final ridge the outlines of the Baltoro Glacier appeared, then faded in a swirl of cloud. Time slipped away. I felt danger in the air—a storm was coming, night was falling. I was dreaming, yet I was not asleep.

Disbelief was my feeling when I broke onto the summit, an icy windswept dome fringed by rocks. I wandered in

circles around that top, stunned to arrive at the place I'd fantasized about for half a lifetime, a place I never truly thought I'd reach. It was windless, soundless, and surprisingly warm under the blanket of cloud. Our smiles were weary. We hugged each other. The feel of my friends made the moment more real. Then, with darkness nearly upon us, we left, staggering down like drunks.

Back at the funnel-shaped couloir, I kicked my crampons and sliced my ice axes into the névé. Pausing to rest, I looked at the sun sinking into western China. I'd watched many sunsets before, but this one was unlike any I'd seen: the sun was far below me.

We fought our way down through powder avalanches and cold. Every fiber in my body ached. An overpowering urge to stop moving, to curl up in the snow and sleep welled up in me. Back in the tent at 8,000 meters, we lay exhausted. We still had far to go before we were out of harm's way, but I remember the happiness of laying shoulder to shoulder with my companions, feeling the fear drain out of me, knowing that K2 had given us the dream and had decided to let us live after all.

Greg Child

Left *American climbers ascend the slopes on the lower part of K2.*

Facing *The summit of K2.*

Photographs by Galen Rowell

The ridge had been attempted by three different expeditions. The first part can be compared to the north face of The Courtes, but with a lot of bore ice. I followed the icy goulottes that led up to 25,262 feet, and then there was a rocky stretch. Between 8,000 and 8,500 meters, we ran into disastrous conditions, windslabs and deep snow. It took twelve hours to get past that stretch. At just a hundred yards short of the summit, it seemed to me entirely unlikely that our climb would be crowned with success. I had sworn to take thirty steps and then stop, but with snow up to my armpits, taking twenty steps at a time was as much as I could do. But I was close, and I could see the peak. The summit was right there, you could reach out and touch it. A magical moment, the last few yards, the final rise. Perhaps a stronger emotion than

what one felt when one finally stood at the top. Success was within reach, and certain. We were overcoming the last few obstacles before setting foot on the summit ridge. It was hard snow, there were no slabs of black ice, there were no impending dangers. There was simply a long ridge to climb without a preying doubt of never reaching the top. The sun was sweetly setting. Slowly, we were overcome by a feeling of intense joy. A simple happiness, the certainty that we would finish. We forgot our weariness, the cold, the prospect of a nighttime descent with only the light from our headlamps. Our minds were filled with one thing only—we had achieved our dream. After climbing this giant, Pierre and I savored these almost surreal moments.

Christophe Profit

63

The Trango Towers
Throne of the Gods

Trango, Uli Biaho, Latok, The Cathedrals are all unfamiliar names to the general public. But over the past twenty years, these rock faces were the arena in which the modern techniques of mountain climbing first appeared in Asia. On the towers that loom over the Baltoro Glacier, Himalayan mountain climbers were transformed from glory-seekers into up-to-date climbers.

The beginning of this adventure arrived unannounced. The Karakoram Range was cordoned off to foreign climbers from 1961 until 1974. During those same years, rock climbing—specifically on granite—became extremely popular at Yosemite, in Patagonia, and in the Arctic. When the area finally was opened again to foreign climbers, there were as many requests to climb the smaller towers as to climb the higher peaks.

In 1975, an attempt by an English team (Mo Anthoine, Ian MacNaught-Davis, Martin Boysen, and Joe Brown) to scale the Nameless Tower—the area's most spectacular—was unsuccessful. The expedition came close to ending in tragedy when Martin Boysen, climbing just 650 feet from the top of the tower, became trapped, his knee jammed into a crack. In order to free himself, he was forced to cut away his trousers—and here and there, bits of skin—until he was finally free.

In 1976, the English team returned, with Malcolm Howells in place of MacNaught-Davis, and this time made it to the top. The following year, an American expedition (Dennis Hennek, Jim Morrissey, Galen Rowell, John Roskelley, and Kim Schmitz) reached the top of the tallest peak in the massif, the Great Trango Tower, 20,528 feet high, crowned by a dizzying pinnacle of snow and ice. Then the expeditions multiplied.

It is not easy to provide a complete roster of them. In 1987 alone, a Norwegian attempt to climb the Second Tower ended in tragedy, and Slovenian climbers scaled the Nameless Tower via a route that included stretches of Grade IX. Shortly thereafter, the Swiss climbers Michel Piola, Stéphane Schafter, Michel Fauquet, and Patrick Delale attempted the twenty-seven pitches of the west pillar on the Great Tower. And, in 1988, the Italian climbers Maurizio Giordani, Kurt Walde, Rosanna Manfrini, and Maurizio Venzo scaled the Tower of Uli Biaho (20,636 feet) by the south pillar, and the Swiss/Polish party led by Erhard Loretan and Wojtek Kurtyka blazed another extreme route up the east face of the Nameless Tower. The route pioneered by the Australian Greg Child and the American M. Wilford in the summer of 1992 on the South Face of the Great Trango Tower was also of a notable level.

On 24 June we reached the overhang and immediately began the waltz on fixed ropes in open air— the zone that we had to cover was beyond vertical for more than three consecutive pitches! An oblique corner was the only possible line of climb. Linear beauty, but also a sure dose of adrenalin! The maddening void over which we dangled (nearly 2,000 feet, plus the yawn of the gully beneath that) is the best indication of just what sort of "big wall" experience we had come in search of. The summit was close at hand. When we reached it, to our good fortune, the weather was gorgeous. K2, Gasherbrum, and Broad Peak stood in array before us. There was still one more challenge—Tchouky (Michel Fauquet) wanted to leap by parachute from the snowcap on the summit. A few marks in the snow, a thrilling moment before an updraft caught him, a few more steps, and then he plunged out of sight. Tchouky took ten minutes to reach base camp, and we got there the next morning.

Michel Piola

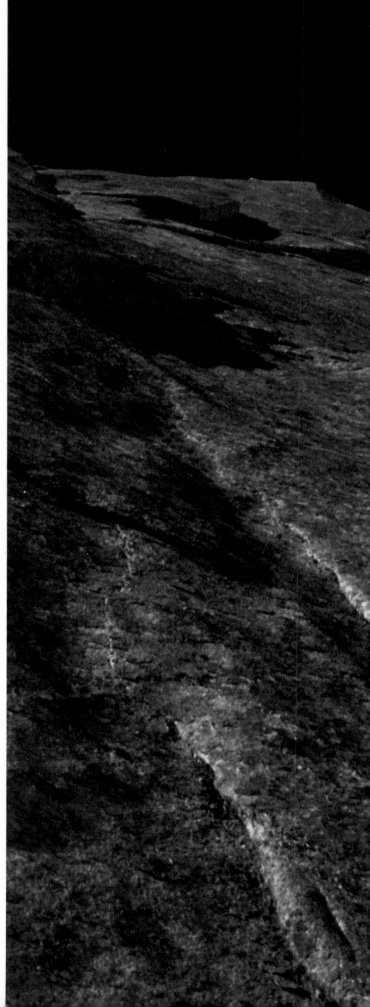

Below *A climber ascends the granite slabs on the west face of Nameless Tower. Photograph by Michel Piola*

Right *The second Trango Tower, the Norwegian Pillar, seen from the snowy north slope. Photograph by Michel Fouquet/Agence Freestyle*

PAGES 68–69
The majestic Trango Towers rear up in all their savage beauty; to the right stands the Nameless Tower. Photograph by Galen Rowell

BEN NEVIS ▲

WETTERSTEIN

CERVINO   EIGER   KARWENDEL

MONT BLANC   OBERLAND   DOLOMITES   GROSSGLOCKNER

NARANJO DE BULNES ▲   OISANS   JULIAN ALPS

PYRENNES   PIZ BADILE

MONTE ROSA   PIZ BERNINA

MONT AIGUILLE

Facing An aerial view of Mont Aiguille, the splendid limestone tower on the Vercors Massif, where mountain climbing had its official birth in 1492. Photograph by Mario Verin

The ice walls of Mont Blanc, Monte Rosa, and the Oberland, the granite towers of Piz Badile and the Chamonix Aiguilles, the amazing limestone formations of the Dolomites, the mountains of Briançon, and the Wilder Kaiser. Among the world's mountains, the Alps may not be the highest or the roughest. But without a doubt, no mountain range on the planet can equal them in terms of spectacular views, variety, and charm.

From Nice to Vienna, from the Mediterranean to Central Europe, the great curving mass of the Alps covers pieces of seven different nations, and can be rightly considered the heart of the continent. Most of what is left of Europe's wilderness can be found in the Alps. The Alps boast sixty-five peaks that tower more than 13,000 feet above sea level. The Alps possess the most beautiful, most challenging, and most difficult peaks on the continent. Three centuries separate the time of Antoine de Ville, the French Captain who first climbed Mont Aiguille in 1492, from the ascent of Michel-Gabriel Paccard and Jacques Balmat, the first climbers to scale Mont Blanc. And two centuries more separate the adventuresome conquest of Mont Blanc (15,771 feet) from the

mountain climbing of today. Now, at the dawn of the twenty-first century, tens of thousands of mountain climbers, rock climbers, skiers, hikers, and tourists crowd the "Playground of Europe."

In the time that separates Edward Whymper and Christian Almer from Reinhold Messner and Christophe Profit, some remarkable individuals have tested themselves against the Alps. The stories of Paul Preuss and Riccardo Cassin, the epic achievements of Walter Bonatti and the elegant climbs of Emilio Comici and Hias Rebitsch have done more than just mark new chapters in the history of the mountains. They have put generations of Europeans into closer touch with nature, the mountains, and the wilderness.

The Alps are not alone. Elsewhere on the Old Continent there are other mountain ranges, not as tall but in some cases equally challenging. From the rocks of the Apennines to the peaks of the Pyrenees and the Olympus range, from the raging gales of Scotland to the storms of Norway and the High Tatras, or Vysoke Tatra, in the Carpathian Range, the mountains of Europe have many different faces.

Oisans
The Wild Heart of the Dauphiné

"*Wilderness*—this English word so difficult to translate into French and yet so rich in meaning." These are words of Gaston Rébuffat, one of the finest mountain climbers of the century. Rébuffat loved the white sun-baked rocks of the Calanques, near his native Marseilles, and he knew Mont Blanc better than most. But his love for the wilderness found a particular focus on a different mountain from Mont Blanc—Oisans.

Solitary and savage, devoid of cable cars and mountain roads, these peaks are dear to the hearts of the French and the Piedmontese, and they remain a secret to all but a few. They boast only one "4,000," only one peak that is at least 4,000 meters tall, a little over 13,000 feet. That is the Barre des Ecrins, a splendid pyramid of ice that stands 13,465 feet above sea level. Even wilder are La Meije, Ailefroide, Pic Sans Nom, and Pelvoux; they are all over 3,900 meters, or 12,795 feet.

Here, in the last few years, all of the latest trends of modern mountain climbing have been introduced: ice waterfalls, extreme skiing, the splendid routes more difficult than Grade VI on the walls around Briançon. In March 1960, the gruelling experience of René Desmaison and his team on the northwest wall of the Olan helped to trigger a series of major winter conquests on the Alps. Since the thirties, the solid granite of the Aiguille Dibona has featured routes of remarkable elegance. There is no need for technical virtuosity, however, to enter the heart and spirit of Oisans. The huge snow gullies, the dizzying and tormented ridges, and the labyrinthine south wall of La Meije offer the most impressive experiences. More than a century ago, men like Edward Whymper, William Coolidge, Christian Almer, and Angelo Dibona passed this way.

But the greatest figure associated with Oisans climbing was certainly Pierre Gaspard, a guide from La Grave, whose brilliant intuition was responsible in 1877 for the conquest of the Grand Pic of La Meije. Christian Almer had declared this climb to be *ummöglich*, or impossible. "Impossible, under current conditions," Henri Cordier wrote to the president of the French Alpine Club, just a few days before Gaspard's successful climb. Neither Almer nor Cordier had counted on Gaspard's remarkable skill and determination. "Finally, foreign guides will stop beating us to the top," Gaspard exclaimed as he made his way up the last, dizzyingly airy passage that leads to the top, at 13,068 feet.

We reached the summit, the difficulties were gone, we were happy, and we thought that at last we were safe and secure. The reality was quite different. Darkness fell upon us suddenly, and the blizzard came rushing on. In the most total darkness I began to descend on the rope with the lurking fear of some hidden crevasse. The wind brought huge waves of snow that hit me incessantly. We were half an hour from the refuge, but to reach it we had to pass over some fairly delicate snow bridges. We decided to wait for dawn. We tried to build a shelter with our hands, feet, and crampons. Our toes no longer answered when called. The snow was covering me; indifferently I allowed it to. In the morning we set off again, but the blizzard offered no respite. From time to time I would kneel to keep from putting too much weight on my poor extremities. And then at last, amidst the snow and gusting winds, we saw the shelter.

Pascal Tournaire

Mont Blanc
The Icy Giant

The setting is Chamonix; the time is 6:00 in the evening on August 8, 1786. The golden light that announces the beginning of sunset was slowly stretching its shadows over the mountains when two tiny specks appeared, very near the peak of Mont Blanc, high above the outline of the Rochers Rouges. Baron von Gersdorf spotted the two climbers through his telescope at 6:12 P.M., just as they climbed up from the Petits Mulets, the last, small boulders before the snow cap of the peak. Eleven minutes later, Jacques Balmat and Dr. Michel-Gabriel Paccard were at 15,771 feet, standing at the highest spot in all of Europe. According to eyewitnesses, the two climbers covered the last few meters one beside the other, like racers crossing a finish line.

Evil times were coming for Europe, but the atmosphere at the summit of Mont Blanc was solemn and stately. Paccard's thermometer showed a temperature of 7.5 degrees below zero Centigrade, and the barometer indicated an altitude of slightly higher than 5,000 meters, though the peak is actually just 4,807 meters above sea level. The sky was clear, the north wind was sharp, and the two climbers surveyed an endless panorama of mountains. The snow was hard but not icy, and the climbers erected a stick to which they attached a red banner, to the delight of the spectators down in the valley below. At 6:47, after thirty-five minutes of chilly glory, they began their descent.

The first leg of the route was a dizzying slide down, braking all the way with their alpenstocks until the tips were chipped and dulled. Then came the crevasses of the great ramp of ice (later dubbed the Ancien Passage), the deep snow of the Grand Plateau, and the maze of deep crevasses of the Jonction, which required a more deliberate pace. Shortly after midnight, Balmat and Paccard were out of danger, among the boulders of the Montagne de la Côte. And there, at 2,800 feet, they bivouacked. Despite the cold clear night, incipient frostbite to their fingers, and the beginning of an eye problem for the doctor, in just four hours the next morning they had returned to Chamonix.

Later the two climbers—Balmat, the Chamonix guide, and Paccard, the young physician—were to quarrel about nearly every detail. Balmat was decorated with a medal of the royal house of Savoy and, supported by the public opinion of the entire valley, claimed that he had reached the peak first, climbed back down to help his companion, and had dragged him up to the top. Paccard's version was precisely the reverse. The dispute was

to capture the imagination and interest of many distinguished historians of mountain climbing, as well as the great author, Alexandre Dumas. Looking back from the vantage point of two centuries later, it seems like a fairly inconsequential quarrel.

The following year, Horace-Bénédict de Saussure, the Genevan scholar and wealthy natural scientist who had organized the ascent—by offering a prize of two guineas to the first man to reach the top—climbed to the summit, accompanied by a personal valet and eighteen mountain guides, among them Jacques Balmat. From then on, the climb became a frequent occurrence. In 1808, a Chamonix woman named Marie Paradis climbed to the peak. And, in the peace that followed Waterloo, the glaciers of Mont Blanc became one of the obligatory stops on the Grand Tour. This was the true beginning of modern mountain climbing.

The rocks of the Petit Dru, August 20, 1955 . . . A single man battled the mountain wall, a daunting challenge. His name was Walter Bonatti, he was twenty-five years old, and he came from near Milan. Over the previous five or six years, his remarkable success at unthinkable climbs had brought him to the attention of the world. When he retired from mountain climbing ten years later, his name had became well known everywhere. But now he was battling against a terrifying obstacle.

If one looks at Mont Blanc from Chamonix, the glaciers that descend from the summit are the most impressive barrier. They are not alone, however. To the left—eastward—of the ice cap on the peak rise the ice slopes of Mont Maudit and Mont Blanc de Tacul. Continuing eastward, the Aiguille du Midi is the first in a proud procession of towering rocks—the Grépon, the Aiguille de l'M, Grands Charmoz, the Aiguille du Plan—a set of names known to every mountain climber on Earth. Aiguille, which in French means needle, is now used commonly in mountaineering to indicate any needle-like formation. Set in the deep cut of the Mer de Glace, Mont Blanc's glacier, the tower of the Aiguille du Dru captures the observer's attention as well as the climber's. Red, sheer, steep, and dizzyingly tall, the rocks of Dru soar straight up for more than 3,000 feet. The mountain is two-headed, and the two peaks—the Grand Dru and the Petit Dru—are separated by a deep cut. The Grand Dru was climbed in 1878 by a team led by the great Valais guide Alexander Burgener, and the Petit Dru was conquered the following year by the Chamonix

It was the first time I had ever fallen in the mountains. It was November 1989, and Andy Parkin and I were trying to climb a very difficult new route on the north face of the Aiguille des Pèlerins above Chamonix. I flew backwards through space after my ice tools ripped out of the thin ice behind a corner on the fifth pitch. I stopped eight meters lower, upside down with my pack cushioning the impact as I slapped into the wall. Andy lowered me to a small ledge where I took an inventory of the damage. I expected more. I could tell there would be bruises later on, but nothing was broken. I climbed back up and finished the pitch.

The climb became an obsession with us. An impossibility in the summer months, thin tongues of ice snake down the wall in autumn and winter, linking together the climbable rock features on the face. It is an austere and hostile place that rarely sees the sun.

For our third attempt we accepted the necessity of spending a night somewhere on the face. The following morning, we reached the Col des Pèlerins, and the end of the route that had been an obsession for both of us for more than two years. It was 8:30 in the evening on April 23, 1992. We had finally made the first ascent of "Beyond Good and Evil."

Marc F. Twight

Both of these two climbs are magnificent. The Dent du Géant is splendid no matter how you look at it, especially from the Col du Géant, which is the best point to start from. In the morning, the west slope covered by the standard route is cold and in shade, which makes climbing it unpleasant and rigid. It is therefore best not to stop but to continue directly to the Rochefort Ridge, the snow of which holds the intense chill of the morning, and where the light on the ridge laced with cornices is truly spectacular.

Gaston Rébuffat

native Charlet Straton. In 1935, Pierre Allain and Raymond Leininger scaled the daunting north wall; in 1952, another redoubtable French team (Lucien Bérardini, Adrien Dagory, Marcel Lainé, and Guido Magnone) conquered the west wall, the tallest and the most appealing. The climb took place in two phases, with an exit to the north wall and a subsequent return from that wall—this caused a fair amount of debate. In 1954, the first uninterrupted ascent took place.

But nothing attracted the sort of attention that focused on Bonatti's daring climb. Like all good Lombard climbers, Bonatti learned the ropes on the Grigne, the jagged limestone towers that loom over Lecco. In 1949, at the age of nineteen, he took part in an extremely challenging repeat of Cassin's climb up the north face of the Grandes Jorasses. Later, his climbs on Mont Blanc were to become legendary: the Pilier d'Angle, a solo climb of the Via Major, the Red Pillar of the Brouillard, and the Central Pillar, the highest rock-climb on the mountain. The other climbers performing famous exploits during the same period were about the same age as Bonatti—René Desmaison, Pierre Mazeaud, Chris Bonington, Michel Vaucher, Gary Hemming, and Andrea Oggioni. But it was Bonatti who took on the greatest and most extreme challenges: the Grand Capucin, a huge piece of rock "so regular and so elegant that looking at it made one dizzy," and the southwest pillar of the Petit Dru, which was "pure structure emphasized by the nightmarish void of the west wall—in brief, a perfect route for a perfect mountain."

Bonatti was a man of action. In 1951, with Luciano Ghigo, he conquered the Grand Capucin after two attempts. He went on to the Dru, but was forced to desist twice. Then he made the solo attempt. After bivouacking for four nights, he was at the base of the most difficult stretch of climbing—a slick concave wall that reminded Bonatti of the apse of a church. A gruelling and acrobatic climb took him into a blind alley. Before him plunged a gully thirty feet deep, and beyond it a small crack led onward. Bonatti pondered his next step. He was determined, desperate, and tough, and so he crafted an "intricate system of knots" on his rope, and then wound up and tossed it, much like a cowboy would a lasso. "And now I am going to leap out into nothing," Bonatti muttered to himself as he prepared to jump. He tensed, sprang, and the rope held. As he recalls it, a hundred thoughts crowded into his mind, each one to be remembered for the rest of his life. Then he made his way upward, driven by the instinct for survival. A few hours later, he reached the summit.

Between the triumph of 1786 and the great and heroic accomplishments of the fifties and sixties, Mont Blanc was the arena for a great many climbers. And it continued—and continues—to be. But Bonatti's two climbs were the most important, the most telling, and most magnificent moments in the history of the mountain. The first of these was the conquest of the colossus of ice, and then the successful climb up the tallest and sheerest walls, made even more difficult by the featureless granite.

In the ensuing two centuries, Chamonix and Courmayeur went from being mountain villages cut off from history and from the outside world to becoming vacation spots for the rich. Once a forsaken stretch of wilderness, the mountain today receives tens of thousands of visitors every day. Lines form on the warm reddish slabs of rock of the Aiguille du Midi, on the snow ridge on the standard route of Mont Blanc, on the paths up to the refuges of Argèntiere and the Couvercle. Roads, cement, and cable cars all bring about a different sort of overcrowding—that of buildings and infrastructure. At last there is talk of a park, operated jointly by the three countries—Italy, France, and the Swiss canton of Valais—that claim a piece of Mont Blanc. Aside from the majesty of nature here, without a doubt the park will be a monument to humankind's strength, courage, and love of adventure.

From 1860 onward, these qualities were found in English mountain climbers—first among them Edward Whymper—who conquered, with the assistance of their excellent Savoy and Swiss guides, the Grandes Jorasses, the Aiguille Verte, Mont Dolent, and the other major peaks in the massif. Particularly remarkable was the 1865 achievement of Melchior Anderegg and Christian Almer; the guides led their clients without crampons up the dizzying sheer ice wall of the Brenva, a considerable feat even by today's standards.

Around 1880, Albert Frederick Mummery and a new generation of guides—Knubel, Lochmatter, Burgener, and Veretz—introduced the new sport of rock climbing, while on the Italian side Emile Rey, the guide of Courmayeur, led other noteworthy climbs. Upon Rey's death, Giosuè Carducci, the great Italian poet and Nobel laureate, wrote an ode in his memory.

It was the conquest of the Dent, in 1882, that sparked the first dispute over the use of "artificial" climbing equipment (iron spikes, chisels, great lengths of rope) by Jean-Jacques Maquinaz on a wall that Mummery had declared to be "inaccessible by fair means."

The achievements of French climbers during the twenties led straight to the great conquests of the thirties. The "triple strike" of the Brenva by Thomas Graham Brown came only slightly prior to the competition for the north wall of the Grandes Jorasses, the most daunting and difficult wall on the entire massif. In 1935, the German climbers Rudolph Peters and Martin Meier made it over the spur leading to Point Croz, followed shortly thereafter by a Swiss-Italian climbing team. In 1938, the great climber Riccardo Cassin, another iron-hard Lombard, led the team that conquered the Walker Spur, the highest and toughest route. We have already discussed the period following the war. Along with other great achievements, the first winter climbs were made, and there was another race to be first up the Jorasses. The winner, just to keep things interesting, was Walter Bonatti.

In 1961, the competition to climb the Central Pillar led to a tragedy. The dead were Pierre Kohlmann, André Vieille, Andrea Oggioni, and Robert Guillame; the survivors were Bonatti, Roberto Gallieni, and Pierre Mazeaud. A few weeks later, a team of English and Polish climbers finally climbed "the highest spire in Europe," outdoing the finest French climbers of the period.

There were other achievements during the seventies, but there was a real leap in quality around 1980. Having trained on low altitude rock faces, without any inhibitions or fears of their surroundings, a new generation conquered the most difficult routes, seeking out "impossible" slabs of rock and vertical frozen waterfalls, leaping from one wall to another at top speed. Michel Piola, a Swiss climber, blazed over 100 extreme rock-climbing routes. Patrick Gabarrou, Giancarlo Grassi, and Gianni Comino introduced the same approach to ice climbing. Christophe Profit, Eric Escoffier, Jean-Marc Boivin and their disciples threw down the challenge of speed climbing. From the north wall of the Droites to the north wall of the Grandes Jorasses, from the "goulottes" of Mont Blanc to Talèfre, Profit invented the mountain climbing of the twenty-first century. "Plus vite!" was the cry—the language of speed is the language of the future on Mont Blanc.

I had resolved that I would avoid getting involved in the preparations for the expedition and therefore went off to Chamonix to climb with Dougal. We were going to attempt a new route on the north face of the Grandes Jorasses. We spent twelve days on the face—twelve glorious days, when the problems of life were reduced to a few feet of ice in front of our noses, trying to hack a platform for a bivouac in ice that was frozen as hard as the rocks it covered, of trying to survive the fury of a winter storm. We did not get up, but it didn't seem to matter—the experience had been well worthwhile, for we had had twelve days of real climbing, uncluttered by politics and commercial pressures.

Chris Bonington

Facing *A climber rappels down from a serac; in the background is the peak of Mont Blanc du Tacul. Photograph by Mark Buscail*

Below *The ice wall that blocks access to Col Maudit is* a harsh test of a climber's ability. Photograph by Patrick Gabarrou/Agence Freestyle

PAGES 84–85
A spectacular winter dawn seen from the Torino Hut. Over this setting looms the Aiguille Noire de Péuterey; *further down stands the Aiguille de la Brenva, with its granite wall. In the distance, beyond the Val Veny, are the Graian Alps. Photograph by Giovanni Pidello*

To our left, the day was dawning. This was the chilliest part of the night, the hour without color or shadow, the hour in which the steel of the ice axe glued itself to the skin of your fingers. We moved past the bergschrund *and climbed the ridge of rocks that emerged from the glacier. High above, the first rays appeared through the notches in the ridge. Frendo cut steps into the traverse, and then I went on to lead. While the rope payed out behind me, I slowly took possession of this realm of stone. I felt a secret joy that came from my well trained body and from my spirit, happy to see a dream come true. I was on Walker Spur. We were two men on a vertical face, who met every so often at the end of a pitch.*

Gaston Rébuffat

The Matterhorn and Monte Rosa
Sentinels of the Alps

"Croz and I raced ahead, charging along madly elbow to elbow. The race ended in a tie. At forty minutes after one in the afternoon, we had the world at our feet. We had scaled the Matterhorn. Hurrah! There wasn't a trace of footprints on the immaculate snow." To English climber Edward Whymper, that was how the most celebrated ascent in mountain climbing history ended on July 14, 1865. Whymper, his guide Michel Croz, and their five fellow-climbers, a mix of Britons and Valais natives, set foot on the 14,692-foot-high summit of the "noblest rock in Europe."

For Whymper, a draftsman and traveler, the Matterhorn had been an obsession for four years. He had attempted the climb seven times, he had dreamed about the mountain, loved it from afar, and written about it. Further down, on the Lion Ridge, an Italian team witnessed the achievement from below. Jean-Antoine Carrel and the other guides from Breuil in turn reached the peak on the 17th, three days later. But Whymper's achievement had a terrible cost. On the way down, on the jagged boulders near the peak, young Hadow slipped, plunged down onto Croz, and tumbled him out into the void. Francis Douglas and Charles Hudson were pulled down to their deaths. Then the rope snapped. Whymper survived, together with the two Taugwalder guides, father and son, of Zermatt. The following day, a rescue squad recovered the bodies at the foot of the grim north wall.

The best known and most challenging mountain in the world of the nineteenth century, depicted on millions—if not billions—of postcards, thousands of paintings, endless prints, drawings, and even foil chocolate wrappers, the Matterhorn has loomed large in the public eye ever since. It has been the setting for such great achievements as the conquest of the ridges of Z'mutt (Mummery and Burgener, 1879), the ridge of Furggen (Mario Piacenza with Pellissier, Gaspard, and Carrel, 1901), and lastly the immense north wall, finally climbed in 1931 by the Bavarian brothers Franz and Toni Schmid. In 1965, Walter Bonatti was to open a route of his own up the same wall. Five years later, Leo Cerruti and Alessandro Gogna were to scale the partly overhanging wall known as the Nose of Z'mutt.

The Matterhorn, with its crumbly rock, is not only the territory of extreme mountain climbers. The two more traditional routes up (the Swiss route being the easier of the two, while the Italian side is steeper) were both equipped with cables shortly after they opened. Each

summer they receive hordes of visitors, led by guides from the Val d'Aosta and the Valais. Further down, Breuil and Zermatt have grown from villages of shepherds and mountaineers into full-fledged cities, and then on into disturbing expanses of cement and coils of ski lift cable. There is nothing, however, that can hamper the enthusiasm of ambitious climbers, and on a mountain that boasts so many world records, speed climbing was bound to develop rapidly. The four ridges of the mountain were traversed in 1970 by two Swiss guides. In summer of 1990, the Val d'Aosta guide Valerio Bertoglio climbed from Breuil up to the summit at 14,692 feet and back down again in 4 hours, 16 minutes, and 26 seconds.

Competition and the urge to set records vanish if you move from the Matterhorn to the icy peaks of Monte Rosa and the other 4,000s that surround Saas Fee and Zermatt. The Weissmies and the Castore, the Allalinhorn and Point Gnifetti are crowded with expert climbers. The Dom—the tallest summit entirely within Swiss borders—the Täschorn, the Weisshorn, the giant east wall of Monte Rosa, all contain some of the most intriguing wilderness settings to be found in Europe.

The truly serious climbs are still those of fifty if not a hundred years ago: the ridge and the north wall of the Lyskamm, the enormous and dangerous east wall, and the area between the Lenzspitze and the Nadelhorn. All of the latest trends of cutting-edge climbing appear here as well—but the most "fashionable" achievement was the four-day climb by Erhard Loretan and Daniel Troillet; in the winter of 1980, the two climbed all of the peaks around Zermatt and Saas Fee, almost all above 4,000 meters.

Unlike Mont Blanc, Monte Rosa can be seen from the Po valley; on a clear day, you can see it from Milan. And, oddly enough, its name has nothing to do with the color pink (*rosa* in Italian)—it is a corruption of a word that means "white" in the local dialect. Here, despite the crowding, one has the impression that not that much has changed since Giovanni Gnifetti, the parish priest of Alagna Valsesia, reached the peak of Monte Rosa after a number of unsuccessful attempts. Or even since a group of seven young men from Gressoney first ventured out onto the enormous Lys glacier in mid-August of 1778. The valley's folktales spoke of a "Lost Valley," a sort of Alpine Shangri-La, luxuriant and tucked away amid the peaks. When they reached the Lys Col, however, they discovered that all that lay beyond was the Valais.

Oberland
The Home of the Ogre

Above *A climber nears an overhang on the limestone walls of the Bernese Oberland, where walls of ice and mixed terrain offer many mountaineering challenges. Photograph by Robert Bösch*

Facing *Heinz and Üli Bühler climb up the Batman Route on the sheer and daunting walls of the Wendenstock. Photograph by Robert Bösch*

The Eiger—or Ogre—the best known and most feared wall in the Alps, looks out over the gentle meadows of the Kleine Scheidegg and the Grindelwald. The north wall of the Eiger is over 5,900 feet high, and it is dotted with some twenty routes. The classic route that zigzags up is not feared as it used to be. For decades, this somber-colored wall, hammered by rock falls and mottled with ice, represented extreme mountaineering at its apex, full of danger, even sometimes suggesting suicidal tendencies.

The first attempts ended tragically. In 1935, the German climbers Mehringer and Sedlmayer died. The year after that, as two German climbers, Kurz and Hinterstoisser, and two Austrian climbers, Angerer and Rainer, were climbing back down after an unsuccessful attempt, Toni Kurz died as he dangled, rappelling, within yards of the rescue team. In June 1938, the Italian climbers Bortolo Sandri and Mario Menti fell to their deaths while attempting the wall. Two months later, the team of Anderl Heckmair, Ludwig Vörg, Heinrich Harrer, and Fritz Kasparek conquered the mountain and put an end to the nightmarish "race." This was a joint Austrian and German expedition, which some British commentators dismissed as a "suicidal escapade" by "Nazi fanatics." This is unfair—the conquest of the north wall of the Eiger was one of the great feats of modern mountain climbing.

The Eiger was not able to shake its gloomy reputation. The first two climbers to attempt a solo climb lost their lives. In 1966, while opening a direct route, the American climber John Harlin fell to his death. According to Tony Hiebeler's 1965 book about the north wall of the Eiger, for fifty-five successful climbs, there were twenty-seven deaths. By 1977, forty climbers had died.

Then record-setting mountain climbing reached the Eiger as well, with the routes opened by Michel Piola in the steepest parts of the wall, the six-hour race up the wall by Reinhold Messner and Peter Habeler, and the one-day ascent of the three great Alpine north walls (Eiger, Grandes Jorasses, and Matterhorn) by Christophe Profit—with the assistance of a helicopter. Behind the Eiger stands the massif of the Oberland, one of Europe's most spectacular pieces of wilderness. Here, seven peaks soar above the 4,000-meter mark. Great pages of mountain climbing history have been written on the Jungfrau, the Mönch, and the Schreckhorn. At the far east section of the massif, the Grimsel slabs are an earthly paradise for athletic climbers.

Above the road through the Klausenpass, there extends a limestone wall that stretches southward. Dozens—maybe hundreds—of routes create a true climber's paradise. You don't need to start early, and you don't need much equipment. I climbed in this heavenly welter of routes with my wife in late autumn once. I returned in December, certain that here I would be able to take an ideal photograph. And that is just what happened. When we reached the final stretch, this perfect layer of white clouds formed below us.
              Robert Bösch

Batman is probably the most difficult and demanding route on the Wenden. Taking a photograph on this wall is a real chore—the first day there were four of us climbing, and we installed fixed ropes; the next day, I photographed Üli and Heinz as they climbed. It was all very fatiguing because during the course of the climb, there was not even one rest spot, and I had to concentrate on each and every handhold to keep from falling. Certainly, the effort expended was amply rewarded—even nowadays, there are not many photographs of routes as difficult, lengthy, and inaccessible as these.

              Robert Bösch

Piz Badile
The Smooth Walls of the Central Alps

Facing *Huge granite slabs distinguish the Cassin Route on the north wall of the Piz Badile, the best known in the Central Alps. Photograph by Marco Milani/K3*

Below *The "Via degli Inglesi," or English Route, opened in 1968, is a highly difficult climb. Photograph by Marco Milani/K3*

The history of the central Alps took a giant step forward from 14 to 16 July, 1937. The northeast wall of Piz Badile, the sheerest and most difficult of the mountains that separate the Valtellina from the Engadine, was finally scaled by two teams of Italian climbers. The three climbers from Lecco—Cassin, Esposito, and Ratti—were one of the finest teams in Europe. The climbers from Como—Molteni and Valsecchi—were decidedly, and tragically, not, and they were to die of exposure on their way down.

Splendid, lonely, and brutal, the peaks that stand at the border between Lombardy and Switzerland are a world of many faces. To the east, the glacial massifs of the Piz Bernina (the easternmost 4,000-meter peak in the Alps) and of Disgrazia are quite tall, spectacular, and alluring, but not particularly difficult. To the west, on the other hand, the granite peaks of Piz Badile, the Cengalo, and the other neighboring peaks are among the toughest summits in the Alps.

The first successful climb up the Badile, which stands 10,852 feet tall, took place in 1918; the climbers were W. A. B. Coolidge and François Dévouassoud. In 1923, the Swiss climbers Risch and Zürcher conquered the north corner, a challenging climb extending well over 3,000 feet. In 1968, three Italian and three Swiss climbers achieved the first winter climb up the northeast wall, with ten bivouacs. During the same period, extreme mountain climbing began to develop on the vast northeast wall and on other nearby walls. Among them, the best known continue to be the Pilastro a Goccia (1976), the Via de Fratello (1970), and the Via degli Inglesi (1968).

On the nearby peaks, one after another the great names in mountain climbing left their signatures—Walter Bonatti, Giusto Gevasutti, Alfonso Vinci, among others. Further down, the enormous slabs of granite in the sunny Val di Mello are the setting for the revolution of the rock climbers—the *sassisti*—of Sondrio. The structures that these climbers discovered and the routes that they employed have been dubbed with fanciful names. One should not take them lightly, however. The Precipizio degli Asteroidi (Asteroid Cliff), L'Oceano Irrazionale (Sea of Unreason), and La Luna Nascente (Rising Moon) are more than just playful names. Cracks and slabs that offer no possible belays are certainly a major step forward in difficulty. Grade VII was developed here, too, before being exported to great walls around the world.

Suddenly I heard a crack, a whistle, and a sort of roar. I looked up and saw a huge boulder breaking loose. I shouted to Esposito to hold the ropes, and I attached myself to the sling and swung under the overhang. At that very moment, the boulder thundered down exactly where I had been hanging, exploding into a thousand pieces and then continuing on its crazy race toward the bottom. The obstacles remained daunting, and we did not have a moment of true safety. We could not take a moment of rest. We absolutely had to continue upwards in order to find a bivouac spot before nightfall.

Riccardo Cassin

The Dolomites
The Pale Mountains

"Beneath us was a terrifying plunge of 650 feet . . . Looking up, the wall juts out a good hundred feet over the base . . . This wall is pitiless. We shall certainly never go back." It was August 28, 1935, and Riccardo Cassin and Vittorio Ratti were halfway up the wall. Mountain climbers had been challenging the Dolomites for more than half a century. From the times of Paul Grohmann and John Ball right up to the times of Tita Piaz and Paul Preuss, the "Pale Mountains" have witnessed hundreds of remarkable exploits. Ten years earlier, the climbs of Solleder and Lettenbauer on the Civetta inaugurated the grand experience of Grade VI.

It was the time of Emilio Comici, Attilio Tissi, Hans Vinatzer, and many other great climbers. The crucial event, however, was the climb of Riccardo Cassin and Vittorio Ratti up the overhanging north wall of the western peak, the most difficult route of the three peaks of Lavaredo; after that achievement, mountain climbing in the Dolomites had an extra dimension, one step beyond the vertical.

Equally split among the Italian provinces of Belluno, Trento, and Bolzano—and, from 1866 until 1918, equally split between Italy and the Austro-Hungarian empire—the Dolomites boast some thirty massifs with fairy-tale shapes, unpredictable moods, and often famous names: Brenta, Marmolada, Civetta, Lavaredo, Sassolungo, Sella, Tofane, Pale di San Martino. With their whimsical shapes and their steep, though not particularly difficult, crags, pinnacles, spires, and chimneys, the Dolomites have always stood as an open challenge to humanity, and not just the mountain-climbing family of humanity. For centuries, shepherds and mountain people have made clever use of ledges and cuts of all sorts. In World War I, the inventiveness typical of blood-thirsty purpose led to the construction of tunnels, roads, and outposts on some of the most difficult and dizzying mountains. The remains of combat on these peaks can still be seen, and they attract an unending stream of visitors.

Among the earliest exploits to grace these mountains were John Ball's climb up the Pelmo (1862), Paul Grohmann's ascent of the Sorapiss (1864), during which the rappel descent was probably invented, and then the conquests of the Marmolada (1864), the Tosa (1865), the Sassolungo (1869), and finally the Croda dei Toni (1870). But things really changed in 1877. During the summer of that year, Luigi Cesaletti, a guide from the village of San Vito, climbed the Torre dei Sabbioni, a subsidiary tower among the massifs of Marmarole and Sorapiss. In the complex and exposed traverses, in the Grade III passages, and in Cesaletti's overt love of adventure, one could already glimpse many characteristics of the mountain climbing of the future.

As early as the final years of the nineteenth century, the Dolomites had become a fashionable tourist spot. For Austrian and German clients, great guides such as Michel Innerkofler, Antonio Dimai, Luigi Rizzi, and Angelo Dibona opened difficult routes on the walls of the Marmolada, the massifs closer to Cortina, and the Brenta. In those same years, however, more athletic types of mountain climbing developed, and the competitions for the conquest of the Campanile Basso of the Brenta and the Campanile di Val Montanaia became the subject of intense interest everywhere. The most famous climber of the day was Paul Preuss—the pure climber, the "solitary knight," the name behind incredible exploits, both in climbing and descending.

On July 28, 1911, Preuss made his most celebrated climb, on the Campanile Basso. With his sister Mina and his friend Paul Relly, he reached the Stradone Provinciale—or Main County Road—as it was jocularly dubbed, a ledge two-thirds of the way up the mountain. He left his sister and friend behind, then traversed solo, on an extremely exposed face, and made his way handhold by foothold up the sheer east wall, until he could scramble onto the ample space of the peak. He made his way back down to where he had left his companions, and then climbed back up to the peak with them following the more traditional route. He left a mark that is still strong and clear in the memories of all those who love and frequent these mountains.

After World War I, the nonmilitary climbers returned to the mountains. Solleder and Lettenbauer's climb up the north wall of the Civetta was followed by the remarkable exploits of Emilio Comici and Riccardo Cassin in Lavaredo, Bruno Detassis's climbs up the walls of the Brenta, the climb of Andrich, Tissi, Faè, and Videsott on the Civetta, and Gino Soldà and Hans Vinatzer's climb up the wall of the Marmolada. This was the "golden age" of classic Grade VI climbing.

Then came World War II, which mercifully spared the valleys of the Dolomites. Following the war, Italy developed, tourism increased, and many high cols and peaks were tamed. The years in which roads, cable cars, and cement attacked the mountain landscape were also the years in which mountain climbing became

The September day dawned bright and beautiful, putting us in good moods, even though we knew that we would soon have to abandon the sun's warm embrace and return into shadow and begin the climb that we had planned for the day. This was the Spigolo Fabbro on Brenta Bassa, a climb of moderate difficulty and therefore nothing out of the ordinary. But the climb we made that day under the guidance of Maurizio Giarolli and Bruno Detassis was unlike anything we had ever experienced. Detassis was pushing eighty, and with youthful enthusiasm he continued his relationship with the mountains, sharing with us his joy at being able to touch once again the friendly rock of the Brenta, intensely experiencing the intimate emotions that every climb, even the simplest, imparts to the climbers. I, a fortunate observer, looked at every detail and breathed in deeply this atmosphere, climbing alongside Bruno and remembering every step and move he made. We climbed calmly and surely, and on a broad ledge halfway up the wall Bruno indulged in a cigar and told us of the adventures of the first climbers to scale the peaks that we could almost reach out and touch: Campanil Basso, Brenta Alta, Cima Tosa, Cima Margherita. A formidable series of walls, corners, fissures, ridges, ledges, and paths, on which he spent his life, performing memorable feats. With great enthusiasm, we set off again, soon reaching the summit where a powerful handshake sealed a day of serene joy.

Adriano Dalpez

Facing *A mountain climber struggles up the Micheluzzi Route on the south face of the Marmolada. Photograph by Alessandro Gogna/K3*

Below, upper *A climber traverses the very difficult Detassis Route on the Brenta Alta. Photograph by Mario Verin*

Below, lower *Bruno Detassis, shown here on the Brenta Dolomites, is one of Italy's best known mountaineers. Photograph by Adriano Dalpez*

An overhanging crack fissure high above us indicated the natural access route to the pillar. I set out, and I immediately found myself obliged to begin driving pitons. Higher up, a hundred feet above my fellow climbers, I had an awkward move to get out of étriers. I stopped at the last step of the étrier, I did everything that I could think of to drive one last little piton, but the rock I could reach was totally devoid of cracks or ledges. It was a classical situation requiring a bolt. Unfortunately, like my fellow climbers, I'd had the good sense to leave them at home. Did that increase the risk? Sure, it did, but it also increased the satisfaction, and the climbing gained in quality—aided- and free-climbing alternated with a harmony equalled only by the beauty of this pillar that never seemed to end.

Alessandro Gogna

increasingly dependent on technology, and especially on pitons. Attention turned once again to the Tre Cime. In 1958, three German climbers (Lothar Brandler, Jorg Lehne, and Dietrich Hasse) and an Austrian climber, Sigi Löw opened a direct route up the north wall of the Cima Grande. The following year, no fewer than three routes were opened on the overhanging north wall of the Cima Ovest.

Clearly, these were incredibly difficult climbs, at the brink of the unsurvivable, which required enormous physical stamina and refined techniques. "We howled out our thirst until it became a hallucination. Our legs were shot with painful cramps," Pierre Mazeaud, one of the climbers who opened the Jean Couzy Route on the Cima Ovest, was later to write. Splendid climbs were made by Walter Philipp and Armando Aste, but the flag-bearer of a renewed devotion to style was certainly Cesare Maestri, "the Spider," who imitated the style of Preuss in climbing the "Via delle Guide" up the Crozzon, the Solleder route up the Civetta, and the Detassis route up the Brenta Alta.

Another climber began his career here—Reinhold Messner, a lad from the Valle di Funes. Messner's *carnet de courses* is too voluminous even to summarize. Let us mention just one date, July 7, 1968, when Messner, together with his brother Günther, attempted the wall of the Sasso della Crusc, overlooking Val Badia. After an uncomfortable bivouac and a long traverse, they had reached the key passage—"a smooth wall, without fissures and practically without handholds." Reinhold tried it, gave up, tried again, and then found "a tiny ledge big enough for fingernails," and up he went. As he later wrote, "I don't know how I got up there, I only know that I found myself on top." At first, not many noticed this climb. The first time it was attempted again was twenty years later, and it was reported to be on the cusp between Grade VII and Grade VIII.

Mountain climbing in the Dolomites has continued to grow. Climbers like Maurizio Giordani, Maurizio "Manolo" Zanolla, and Heinz Mariacher climb up extreme routes that are quite exposed on the Marmolada and other, smoother walls. Their shoes are better, their technology is more refined, and there is a little more protection. And all of them are the heirs to that impulsive and impossible climb of Messner's.

The Julian Alps
Stern Massifs of Limestone

Below *Two climbers dare a frozen waterfall on Prisojnik on the Slovenian side of the Julian Alps. Photograph by Janez Skok*

Facing *Tomo Cesen climbs the Sphinx Route up the north wall of the Triglav. Photograph by Janez Skok*

On clear days, the snowy peaks are visible from Trieste and from the coast of Friuli. Tall, jagged, and grim, the Julian Alps feature the most serious and savage massifs in the Alps. They mark the eastern end of the procession of limestone mountains that begins on the west with the Dolomites. Here, over the past millennia, the German- and Italian-speaking worlds have found a meeting point with the culture of the Slavs. It is no accident that these mountains should have had as their first explorer a poet and mountain-lover whose nationality is difficult to establish.

Julius Kugy was born in 1858 in Gorizia, and grew up on the slopes of the Carso. In 1915 he volunteered—though as a noncombatant, given his age—in the Austro-Hungarian army. Before the war, however, he devoted himself to the Julian Alps. Together with Italian comrades, friends from Carinthia, and Slovenians, he scaled all of the principal peaks dozens of times, and opened routes that were rarely very difficult but were invariably interesting and adventuresome. "The Mangart is the most evocative, the Jôf Fuart is the most luminous, the Canin is the strangest and richest in shades, while the Montasio is the largest and most impressive." With these words, in his book *From the Life of a Mountain Climber*, Kugy introduces us to the aristocracy of the Julian Alps.

The more technological mountain climbing in the Julian Alps shares this quality of being at a meeting ground. Between the two world wars, great climbers of the Dolomites such as Paul Aschenbrenner, Celso Gilberti, Angelo Dibona, and Emilio Comici, took part in the challenge along with Slovenians climbers such as Jaka Cope and Miha Potoćnik. Mira Märko Debekova and Paula Jesih were in all likelihood the first women in the whole of the Alps to lead teams on new routes at levels of Grade V and VI.

After World War II came the Cold War and the sealing off of the border between Yugoslavia and Italy, cutting off access to many of the best mountains. Remarkable climbs ensued on the Jôf Fuart, the Travnik, and on the Triglav, which the Italians continue to think of as the Tricorno. The stomping grounds for extreme mountain climbers in the range became Fusine, a savage arena which looms, with its sheer walls, over the most romantic and wild zones of the forest of Tarvisio. Vertical, icy even in summer, and remarkable to behold, the walls of the Mangart, of the Vèunza, and especially of the Little Mangart di Coritenza are an irresistible challenge. The first routes, in 1931, were the inspiration of Celso Gilber-

ti. The 1941 route, opened by Cirillo Floreanini and M. Kravanja, was compared by later climbers to the Solleder route up the Civetta. Then came even tougher routes (four climbs around Grade VI), all blazed by Ignazio Piussi and his taciturn fellow Friulian climbers, mostly miners or ex-miners. They were outdone, however, by a remarkable exploit of 1970. Enzo Cozzolino, 22, a phenomenon from Trieste, was the first—with A. Bernardini—to climb the great corner of the Little Mangart, which today bears his name. This route covers 2,600 feet, long stretches of Grade VI climbing, crumbling rock below, more solid rock up high, and is, all in all, one of the toughest routes in the Alps.

In 1982-1983, another great Italian mountain climber, Renato Casarotto, was to come back alone in the winter to try the route. It took eleven days of tough and chilly struggle. "My toughest winter climb," he was to say later. The Italian climbers were not the only ones, however. Confined in the fifties and sixties to "their" walls of Raźor, the Jalovec, the Skrlatica, and the Spik, the Slovenian climbers returned to the spotlight later. Today, the best known of them is Tomo Cesen, from Kranj, who did a solo climb in 1990 up the southern wall of Lhotse. Other mountaineers, such as Francek Knez and Janez Skok, climbed Cerro Torre and the Trango Towers, carrying the new flag of Slovenia to the peaks of the tallest mountains in the world.

In 1980, Nejo and I climbed the Obraz Sfinge route up the north wall of the Triglav. We were quickly shrouded in a fog so thick that we could do nothing but climb like blind men, following the line of pitons left in the wall. About halfway up, we heard some voices, but the visibility was so poor that we could not see anyone. We soon met with the person who had cried out: it was Marjon, who had just completed the first solo ascent of Raz Sfinge.

Tomo Cesen

The Austrian Alps
The Gardens of Rock Climbing

Left *A climber takes on the sheer walls along the Locken vom Hocker Route on the Schüsserkarspitze in the Wetterstein Massif. Photograph by Heinz Zak*

Facing *Heinz Zak makes his way past an overhang on the Wilder Socken Route up the Pantherkopfl in the Wetterstein Massif. Photograph from the Heinz Zak Archives*

Huge glaciers, green valleys, and fantastic *klettergartens* ("climbing gardens") are just some of the features of limestone climbing. Much beloved by Austrians and Germans, little known to French and Italians, the mountains of the Tyrol, Carinthia, and the area around Salzburg are among the most beautiful and varied in Europe.

The relatively easy peaks of the Grossglockner and Gross Venediger were some of the first parts of the Alps to have been scaled by humans. On the walls of the Karwendel, the Wetterstein, and the Wilder Kaiser, rock climbing has made a great deal of progress. To the south, the peaks that close the valleys of Stubai and Ziller mark the border with the Italian South Tyrol. To the east, the vast peaks of the Hohe Tauern are entirely set in Austria. The Gross Venediger, surrounded by expanses of glaciers, was first scaled in 1841 by a group of twenty-six climbers. As early as 1800, the Grossglockner (at 12,457 feet, the tallest mountain in Austria) had been climbed, affording a splendid view of the Pasterze glacier. The first climbers to top the Pallavicini Couloir did so in the nineteenth century as well; this is one of the best known ice routes in the Alps, reaching a steepness of up to fifty-five degrees and exposed to frequent rockfalls. With only a few rare exceptions, however, the icy giants of Carinthia and the Tyrol are good-natured mountains, well suited for skiing in the spring.

The real adventure comes in climbing the sheer walls of limestone. In many cases, the history of these solid rocks and crags—along with that of the Alps of Berchtesgaden, in nearby Germany—is a clear forerunner of mountaineering in the Dolomites. In order to see this clearly, all one needs to do is to take a look at the Wilder Kaiser, the most raw and savage range of all, clearly visible to modern motorists from the highway that links Innsbruck with Munich. Here, amidst grazing mountain goats and pleasant grassy valleys, stand vertical sheer walls of diabolically smooth limestone, cut here and there by characteristic vertical fissures.

In 1886, a German student named Georg Winkler climbed a nightmarish chimney of some 1,500 feet on the west wall of the Totenkirchl, and in the following year he repeated the feat on the tower in Vajolet that now bears his name. At the turn of the century, Georg Leuchs accomplished other great deeds. Then came other climbers—Hans Fiechtl, Hans Dülfer, and the famous guide from the Fassa Valley, Tita Piaz. The fact that the first two are remembered as the inventors of the rock piton and the traverse on rope, now known as "tyrolean," is some indicator of the level of technological progress at the time. We should not forget routes such as the one up the west wall of the Predigstuhl and the Onkel Fickel Riss up the Totenkirchl (both of these routes were led by Fiechtl, and the latter is a Grade VI climb), nor should we overlook the great achievements of Dülfer, such as the east wall of the Fleischbank or the direct route up the west wall of the Totenkirchl.

In the thirties, the noteworthy climbs on the Kaiser and other nearby peaks (in particular the Wetterstein) were achieved by climbers such as Fritz Wiessner, Peter Aschenbrenner, and Roland Rossi. It was Mathias "Hias" Rebitsch, a Tyrolian born in Brileg—even today virtually unknown outside of Germany and Austria—who first hit Grade VII on the walls of the Fleischbank. On the Maukspitze in 1943, nineteen-year-old Hermann Buhl, later the first man to climb Nanga Parbat, completed "the most difficult ascent in his entire career of mountain climbing."

The fifties and sixties were years of phenomenal growth in the numbers of mountain climbers, and in the number of climbs whose importance was in some sense diminished by the use of pitons. The first instances of free-climbing in the seventies took place on the Kaiser and later became a craze on the Marmolada. Then Heinz Mariacher (born in the nearby village of Wörgl), Luggi Rieser, Reinhard Schiestl, Heinz Zak, Helmut Kiene, and Reinhard Karl went on to attain the level of Grade VII repeatedly, continuing the march of progress onward and upward. Michael Hoffmann, of Munich, scaled a number of Grade VIII routes, while Wolfgang Mueller and Luggi Rieser opened the way for Grade IX.

Just as everywhere else, there ensued a number of discussions concerning style of climbing, use of pitons, and ethics. "I am slightly disappointed that walls this rich in history and charm should increasingly become a giant jungle gym for athletic climbers," wrote Mariacher in 1989, in the Italian magazine, *Alp.* "The avant-garde has never yet allowed itself to be influenced by disputes," answered Andreas Kubin. The years pass, the ropes change, along with the pitons and the shoes, but the sheer limestone of Austria remains the arena of the future for European rock climbing.

"Put the same old foot into the same old footprint." I often think of this folk saying when, for the thousandth time, we climb the same old route up the south face of the Schüsselkarspitze. Despite the numerous tempting climbs and the obligatory routes for extreme mountaineers on the sheer walls of the Alps, this slick yellow-and-gray wall, 1,300 feet tall and made of the finest limestone of Wetterstein, always draws me back. Slabs worn by water, ledges full of cavities, cracks that vary continually, on a solid and secure, almost friendly rock. In 1989, Thomas Nagles and I climbed the "Leben in Sonnenschein" route, Grade IX and higher, along a wall that was slick and slippery as an eel. We had to climb hanging from some very precarious skyhooks.

Heinz Zak

Ben Nevis
Glittering Armor of Ice

Moors and castles, jagged rocks and wind-swept fjords— Scotland, the "land of mountains and tides" so dear to Sir Walter Scott—has always captured the imagination of travelers from other parts of the world. For nearly a century, however, travelers and climbers in the Alps were completely unaware of the achievements and even of the mountains challenging British climbers. There was general admiration for the British when they came to the continent to climb the Matterhorn or the Grépon, to found the Alpine Club, or to show the way up Everest. But the damp, dark rocks of Britain were completely ignored. History tends to repeat itself—the granite cliffs of Yosemite would shift in a few years from provoking indulgent smiles to becoming legendary climbing spots.

It was the amazing exploits of the sixties that alerted the world to the progress of British mountain climbing. The climbers—Don Whillans, Tom Patey, Chris Bonington, and Joe Brown—attained their skill at rock climbing on the steep walls of the Lake District, Cornwall, and Wales. But their tenacity, their ability to withstand gales, and above all their refined ice-climbing techniques, all come from the walls of Scotland.

In the summer, Ben Nevis is a popular destination for outings, both via the south trail and via the savage valley of Allt'a Mhullin, along which one can easily observe the walls of the mountain. These walls, as tall as 1,300 feet in places, are imposing in stretches (in particular, the Càrn Dearg, a spur with a number of extreme routes), though they are not particularly difficult for those who know the Alps well. The big surprise comes in the winter. It is difficult to smile at Ben Nevis and its 4,406 feet of altitude from December to April, or for that matter, at any other of the 543 Munros, the Scottish peaks that are higher than 3,000 feet, named after Sir Hugh Munro. The north wind blows directly from the Arctic, transforming the walls of Ben Nevis, of the Cairngorms, and of the mountains that straddle the pass and valley of Glencoe and the Cuillins of Skye into glittering icy suits of armor.

The history of winter mountain climbing on Ben Nevis ("Nevis" in Gaelic means "diabolical" or "infernal") began around 1800 with the exploits of Norman Collie and his fellow climbers—the ascent of Tower Ridge in 1892 is considered by many the official inauguration of mountain climbing in the area. From 1896 until 1921, Harold Raeburn—a name never heard on the Alps— blazed dozens of routes over ice that were far more difficult than the routes up Mont Blanc during that period.

With a number of remarkable climbs to his credit in the Caucasus, and good efforts on Kanchenjunga and Everest, Raeburn pioneered twelve new routes up Ben Nevis. From Observatory Ridge, covered in the summer of 1901, he also accomplished the first winter ascent, in 1920. In the thirties, Bill Murray, Graham MacPhee, and others continued his achievements.

In the fifties and sixties, the important, practically vertical routes of Ben Nevis were all scaled. The most noteworthy—Point Five Gully—was climbed in 1957 after a series of attempts which sometimes ended in tragedy. One stormy morning, Tom Patey, Hamish MacInnes, and Graeme Nicol made their way laboriously up from the CIC Hut, the small refuge that can be reached from Fort William at the base of the route. The first stretch, which is nearly vertical, was climbed by MacInnes, the best known Scottish climber in history. Then came an easy stretch, then a vertical stretch, where MacInnes carved "steps worthy of a Yeti" with his heavy ice axe. Then the slope became less steep again. "At that point, we had made our way through the forest of sheer ice walls, and the way was clear to the summit ridge."

Other struggles, storms, and adventures ensued in the ascent in 1959 up Point Five Gully (Alexander, Clough, Pipes, Shaw) and in 1965 of The Curtain (Knight and Bathgate), all of which were climbed with old-fashioned ice axes and normal crampons. Then, thanks to the new toothed and ultra-short ice axes invented by Hamish MacInnes in his workshop in Glencoe, the gullies became less dangerous and progress safer and more expeditious. The challenge shifted to winter climbing of the open walls of the summer rock routes, which are covered by inches of ice in the winter.

The best examples of this new trend were the first winter ascents of Carn Dearg Buttress on Ben Nevis. In 1974 Mick Fowler and Victor Saunders climbed the Shield Direct. Twelve years later, Kenny Spence and Spider McKenzie conquered Centurion, which for the Sixties generation had always been a major challenge, even in summer conditions.

Scotland in the seventies was the source of the idea of frontpoint climbing on ice, which rapidly made its way to the Alps. Today, the once little-known Highlands receive winter visits from nearly all the best Alpine ice climbers.

The following day we climbed Five Point Gully, a superb icy gully with stretches as steep as ninety degrees, which leads to the peak of Ben Nevis. At the top, the wind was curving the rope, and you could just make out the sun in an Arctic whirlwind of phenomenal proportions. We were pleased at our success, and so the next day we climbed Zero Gully, even more demanding, the most famous and beautiful winter climb on Ben Nevis. I remember the first pitches— the ice was thin and the climb quite treacherous. The morning after, we were at the beginning of a broad gully, beneath the superb wall of Creagh Meaghaidh. Suddenly, a blanket of snow broke loose. I remained anchored exactly where I hung, but the snow hurtled down upon my climbing companion and swept him away. That day, Smith's Gully was none too gentle with us. Each pitch involved at least sixty-five feet of sheer vertical climbing, and the grim gully was swept by continual avalanches of powdery snow. At the summit, visibility was nil. It was night by the time we got back to our little van, tottering.

Alessandro Gogna

At the beginning we climbed an ice slope, none too steep, which then narrowed, becoming increasingly vertical, until it had turned into a waterfall, set between vertical walls, and in the end blocked off by a sheer wall, formed by a boulder lodged in the gully. This was the first obstacle. I was wedged in the cave formed by the boulder—it was like being in a refrigerator. Hamish set to work on the ice walls beneath the sheer drop towering above us. It took us an hour and a half to clear the passage. The next obstacle was far worse. Hamish untied himself, tossed the rope around a boulder, and set off again, cutting steps for hands and feet. The water splashed him, wetting him to the bone. A grunt of relief, and he managed to hoist himself up the wall, far from the rushing water.

"Aren't your feet cold, Hamish?"

"No, I can't feel them at all. It's a splendid climb, isn't it?"

Chris Bonington

Naranjo de Bulnes
The Iberian Monolith

Left *The distinctive shape of Naranjo de Bulnes looms 8,264 feet over the wild valleys below. Photograph by Pérez de Tudela*

Facing *A mountaineer ascends Naranjo de Bulnes, the emblem of Spanish mountain climbing. Photograph by Pérez de Tudela*

Spain is more than just sunny beaches and arid plains. In Andalusia, the easy-to-climb, snowy peaks of the Sierra Nevada serve as a backdrop to the Alhambra. To the northeast, the savage range of the Pyrenees separates Catalonia, Aragon, and the Basque Provinces from France. The tallest peak in that range is the Pico de Aneto, which soars over 11,000 feet. And all over the Iberian peninsula, whimsically shaped mountains and peaks—Montserrat, the Mallos de Riglos, the peaks of the Sierra de Gredos and those of the Pedriza de Manzanares—loom proud and unopposed over the landscape.

Spanish mountain climbing, however, has quite another symbol. To the north, in Asturias, stands the splendid and untamed group of mountains known as the Picos de Europa, in the Cantabrian Range. This group of limestone formations boasts one of the most spectacular monoliths in all of Europe. Spanish climbing had its birth here—on the Naranjo de Bulnes. The peak reaches a height of 8,264 feet, overlooking raw and desolate valleys. To the north and the south, it possesses rounded walls that soar close to 1,000 feet straight up from the ground. The west wall is twice as high. At the turn of the century, it was conventional wisdom that the Naranjo was impossible to climb.

"What a miserable reputation my fellow Spaniards and I would have if one day foreign mountain climbers were to plant their flag on the peak of Naranjo de Bulnes, in the heart of my favorite place to hunt chamois." So mused Don Pedro Pidal in a diary entry of 1904. Don Pedro, Marquis of Villaviciosa de Asturias, had only one answer to these doubts. On 5 August of that year, together with Gregorio Perez, a guide from the nearby village of Cain, Don Pedro climbed the northeast wall. To reach the peak, the pair of climbers overcame severe difficulties; they climbed down without pitons or ropes, with the exception of a brief stretch where they left one rope behind them. Two years later, a German climber named Gustav Schulz climbed to the peak, but the honor of Don Pedro was safe. In 1924, Victor Martinez Campillo scaled the Naranjo along the south wall, now considered to be the normal route.

In Spain, modern mountain climbing developed in the fifties and sixties. In 1962, Ernesto Navarro and Alberto Rabadá, natives of Aragon, succeeded in climbing the daunting west wall in just five days. The following year, the two climbers died on the north wall of the Eiger. In 1973, the first winter climb of the west wall was covered with great public interest by television and

the press; this was unprecedented in Spain. In 1974, a group of mountain climbers from Murcia, led by Miguel Angel Gallego, opened a direct route up the west wall. Later, another fourteen routes were added, and eight of them were credited to Gallego and his brothers. Among all of those routes, particular mention should go to "Sueños de Invierno." José Luis and Miguel Angel Gallego decided in 1983 to climb past the hardest part of the wall without using bolts. In order to do this, they took sixty-nine days, during which time they never left the wall, sleeping on hammocks at night. This exploit, which is more of a spiritual exercise than an athletic achievement, took place in winter; it is unlikely that this record will soon be beaten.

Not everything is extreme on Naranjo, however. The dozens of routes up the extremely solid limestone on the mountain are followed each summer by hundreds of climbers. Climbers led the public outcry at the beginning of the eighties that opposed the projects to deface the Picos de Europa with new roads and cable cars. Spain is thus in the vanguard of environmentally pure treatment of the mountains as well.

Winter 1973. Television, radio, the press—they were all present to cover the three "rival parties" that were racing for the summit. We were moving slowly along the sheer wall. Airplanes and helicopters buzzed around us, taking pictures. I have remarkable recollections of those days, so vital to Spanish mountain climbing. Before me stretched a "major climb." I did not even want to look at it, but I knew that I had to make that climb, even though I felt clumsy and tired. I was hanging over the void, and I saw small ledges in the rock. Where you can barely fit the tips of your fingers is where there is technique and courage. Antonio belayed me carefully, and then it was as if fifteen years fell away from me. I stretched and contracted on the tiny handholds, and I felt agile and competent. Fear hid somewhere around the corner. The fireworks, the laurel wreaths, the ancient dances of Asturias held in our honor, the welcoming committees, the crowds and the journalists— nothing like this had ever happened because of a climb. We mountain climbers were not accustomed to being feted like bullfighters or sports heroes.

César Pérez de Tudela

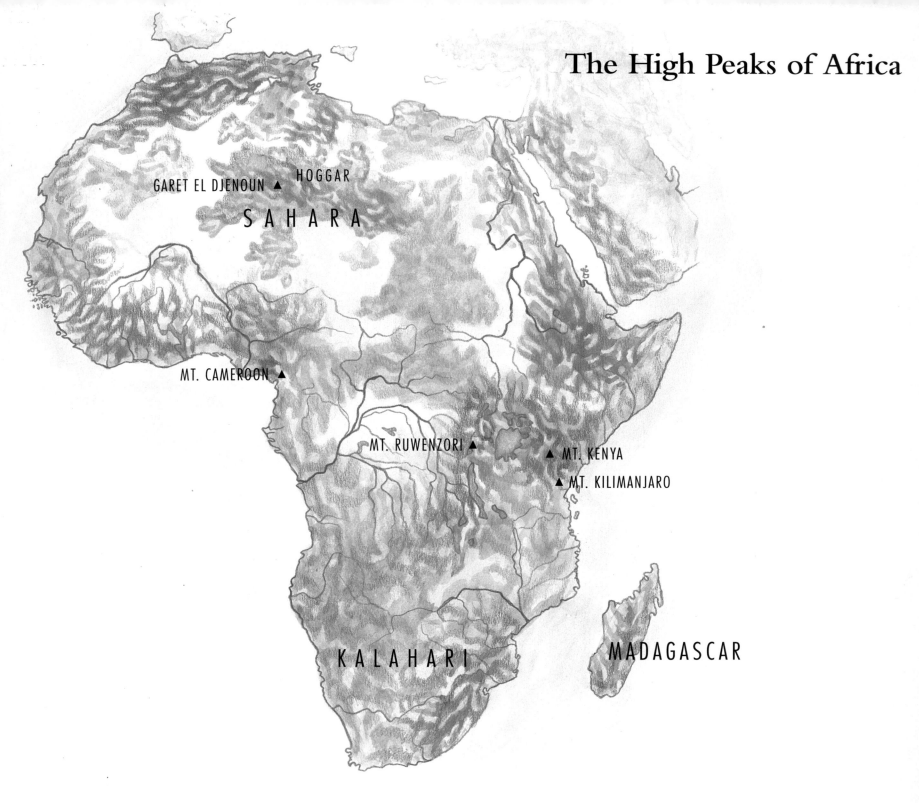

GARET EL DJENOUN ▲ HOGGAR

S A H A R A

MT. CAMEROON ▲

MT. RUWENZORI ▲   ▲ MT. KENYA

▲ MT. KILIMANJARO

K A L A H A R I   M A D A G A S C A R

Facing Catherine Destivelle, one of the finest European climbers, makes her way up treacherous cliffs near Bandiagara in Mali. Photograph by Gérard Kosicki

The vast mineral expanse of the Sahara, the steaming rain forests of the Congo. The tropical coasts of Zanzibar and the Gulf of Guinea, and the mighty streams of the Zambezi and the Nile. Lions, elephants, zebras, and antelopes. Palm trees, acacias, and elephant grass. The scorching sun and the sudden rains. The lush bottom of the Red Sea. Of all the continents on the planet, Africa is richest in attractions for those who love nature. Only rarely, however, does anyone think of the Dark Continent as a land of mountains. Still, there are definitely high peaks there. They are separated by great distances, but there are many, and they are wild and incredibly varied.

Only a few of the African ranges are attractive to ice and rock climbers. To the north, the rounded, seldom jagged peaks of the Atlas Range mark the transition from the Mediterranean region to the vastness of the desert. These are mountains best suited for trekking and expeditions on horseback. Surprisingly similar are the attractions of the Ethiopian ambas. Some of the most amazing trails in the world can be found in the Virunga Mountains—the gorilla-inhabited volcanoes in Zaire, Rwanda, and Uganda—and on Mount Cameroon, the tallest in West Africa. Still further south, other peaks

loom over the deserts, such as South Africa's Drakensberg Mountains or the mountains of Namibia. Tamanrasset and the Hoggar Mountains, with their surreal spires, each year attract hundreds of European climbers.

The heart of mountain climbing in Africa, however, beats for the continent's three tallest peaks—Mount Kilimanjaro, Mount Kenya, and Mount Ruwenzori. Ruwenzori, actually a mountain group, stands on the border between Zaire and Uganda. Here, one can have remarkable adventures in the forests and enjoy brief climbs over dark rocks and bizarre sculptures of ice. Mount Kenya, which soars to over 17,000 feet, offers a selection of routes capable of attracting even the most demanding climbers. And lastly, Kilimanjaro, close to 20,000 feet, with its huge steps of ice looms over the savannah.

"As wide as all the world, great, high, and unbelievably white in the sun." With these words, Ernest Hemingway described the mountain over fifty years ago in his short story "The Snows of Kilimanjaro." A dream? Perhaps. But a dream towards which 10,000 dedicated climbers strive each year.

The Sahara
The Spirit Mountains

The black shade of the huge mountain climbed rapidly eastward, cutting through the distant haze with its black sword of shadow. Everything moved with a surreal rapidity, the obscure cones of the distant peaks stretching and darkening; as the light died out, the wind stiffened, increasing the impression of movement. The wind whipped along the smooth granite wall, spiraling around us, charged with the last warmth being scattered through the nocturnal chill. The impression that we were riding a great spirit, charging madly through the wind and cold, became stronger and stronger, the Garet el Djenoun, the mountain of spirits of the Tuareg people, a whirlwind of whistles and murmurs, light and shade, heat and cold, appeared to us up there with all its disquieting force.

Mario Verin

"A large, dark-blue motor coach stands in the middle of a street in Algiers. Before it stand a dozen or so passengers. On the sides of the bus, the destinations of the voyage are written in black letters." It was April 2, 1935, and what seems like the beginning of an adventure story is just the first step—some 2,000 miles away from the peaks—in the foundation of a mountain climbing tradition in Saharan Africa. The bus described above carried Roger Frison-Roche, a guide from Chamonix and the author of some of the best selling books on mountains ever published.

The real star of this story, however, was a mountain in the massif of Tefedest, some 250 miles from Tamanrasset, the "Capital of the Tuaregs." In the Tuareg tongue, this peak is the Garet El Djenoun, the "Mountain of Spirits." On April 15, however, the djenoun of the desert had very little success in warding off the technique and determination of Frison-Roche and his climbing companion, Captain Raymond Coche. At 7:30 that morning, the two climbers successfully overcame the last, difficult passages. They ascended an exposed stretch, a slab of crumbling rock, and a ledge where a wild olive tree grows, then experienced the giddy joy of reaching the peak, at 7,644 feet. "We were sailing through the heart of Atlantis, on the most monstrous vessel that our imaginations could have dreamed up," wrote Frison-Roche in his book, *Carnets Sahariens*.

In 1881, during the time of Mummery and Winkler, one of the first European expeditions to visit the area was slaughtered by the Tuaregs. In 1916, a group of Libyan rebels on Assekrem, on the massif of Hoggar, killed the Belgian Charles de Foucauld. It was not until much later that Europeans found easy, safe access to the deep south of Algeria. In the thirties, French expeditions scaled the peaks of Morocco's High Atlas range, where the Toubkal soars to 13,734 feet.

There was little doubt, however, that the most inspiring challenges lay further to the south, in the heart of the Sahara, among the reddish spires and surreal but entrancing shapes of the Saharan ranges of Tassili n'Ajjer, the Hoggar, the Tefedest, and the Air. It was Frison-Roche and his companions who opened the way to this unknown land. Before World War II, a few others returned, among them the Swiss climber Edouard Wyss-Dunant and the French climber Alain de Chatellus. At the end of the fifties, another halt to climbing was imposed by the Algerians' war of inde-

Facing *A team climbs the Clocher du Tezoulag, a spectacular peak in the Hoggar Massif of Algeria. Photograph by Didier Givois*

Below *The smooth slabs of Mont Elephant, in the Mesnou Massif, make difficult climbs possible in a spectacular African setting. Photograph by Mario Verin*

pendence from France. After the war, the border opened again, and it was, ironically, French climbers who blazed the greatest number of routes. Among the most famous episodes was the conquest in 1966 of the Takouba. The climbers were Pierre Mazeaud and Lucien Béraradini; the enterprise was filmed by Pierre Vernadet. Other remarkable achievements worthy of mention were the French and the Italian routes on the Saouinan ("The Hand"), the longer and more daunting climbs up the Tahoulg Sud, and the extreme routes blazed up a number of different walls by the Spanish teams of José Anglada and Miguel Angel Gallego.

Each winter—the nicest season in the Sahara—new conquests are added. The largest desert in the world is just a three-hour flight from Europe. From Algeria and Libya to Niger and Mali, hundreds of granite, sandstone, and lava spires await their first conqueror. It is difficult to believe that the adventure of Saharan climbing will ever come to an end. The djenoun will always have a place to call home.

Kenya, Kilimanjaro, Ruwenzori
The African Queens

Left *The Nelion Wall, seen from Point Lenana, stands out against the morning light. The standard route up Mount Kenya wends through the rocks on the left. Photograph by Stefano Ardito*

Facing *A climber rappels down a wall on the standard route on the Nelion Wall, a pleasurable Grade III or Grade IV climb. Photograph by Galen Rowell*

"Arriving in a west African town with an ice axe, climbing boots, and several hundred feet of rope seemed for some reason ridiculous." So began Eric Shipton's African adventure in 1929. Shipton, an English mountain climber, reached Kenya before his twenty-second birthday. In the following half-century, Shipton was to climb in Patagonia, on Nanda Devi, and from the slopes of Everest to the lesser-known peaks of China. Shipton earned a reputation as a formidable traveler, an adventurer, ice and rock climber, and an extraordinary explorer of mountains.

Mount Kenya was Shipton's first exploit outside of Europe. Together with Percy Wyn Harris, he attempted to climb Batian, at 17,058 feet, the massif's highest, from the northeast, and then finally reached it after climbing over the peak of the Nelion, only forty-five feet lower. The following year, with Bill Tilman, he climbed the long and difficult west ridge of the tallest peak. Men had been climbing mountains in Africa for at least half a century, but it was the adventures of Shipton and his companions that gave African climbing a sporting dimension.

At its outset, the history of the three greatest mountains (Kenya of course, and Kilimanjaro, at 19,340 feet, and Ruwenzori, at 16,790 feet) is a history of exploration and debate. In 1848, a Swiss missionary named Johann Rebmann, the first European to report seeing the snows of Kilimanjaro from afar, was treated as a madman once he returned to Europe. In 1888, a great name in African exploring—Henry Morton Stanley— was the first modern European to see the Mountains of the Moon (as they were dubbed by Ptolemy), the Ruwenzori Range, that separates the muggy rainforests of Zaire and the Congo from the green hills of Uganda.

As if by magic, mountain climbers showed up. After a few attempts by explorers, the German cartographer Hans Meyer and the celebrated Austrian mountain climber Emil Purtscheller finally reached the summit of Kilimanjaro in 1889 and dedicated it to the German Kaiser. Ten years later, two guides from Courmayeur, César Ollier and Joseph Brocherel, climbed with a Scotsman, Sir Halford Mackinder, to the highest peaks of Mount Kenya, and dedicated them to the Masai chiefs Batian and Nelion, naming Point Lenana after the son of one of the chiefs. When Luigi Amedeo di Savoia, the Duke of the Abruzzi, climbed the peaks of the Ruwenzori in 1906, he was more conventional in his dedicatory choices. Climbing in the company of men from Mont Blanc, he reached the highest peak and named it Point Margherita, after the queen of Italy; the second highest peak became Point Alexandra, after the queen of England, wife of Edward VII.

The climb up Kilimanjaro was a fatiguing hike at high altitude; scaling Ruwenzori involved some far-from-easy ice climbing; scaling Mount Kenya entailed stretches of difficult to severe rock climbing. Between the two world wars, some rather more technical climbing was done on the "queens of Africa." After Shipton's admirable exploits, German climbers went on to challenge the sheer ice of Kilimanjaro, while Belgian climbers opened some very difficult routes up the dark rocks of Ruwenzori. Then the three mountains fell into three radically different roles. Kilimanjaro, high and easy, celebrated by the famous American author Ernest Hemingway, became one of the most popular destinations for trekkers from all over the planet. Each year, thousands climb it. Ruwenzori, on the other hand, remains distant, secret, mysterious. Partly because of the incessant rains and partly because of the political turmoil that shrouds Uganda and Zaire, this mountain keeps the intriguing aura of great adventure.

Serious climbers turn their eyes to Mount Kenya. Climbers from Nairobi, along with some of the finest European and American mountaineers, take turns blazing difficult routes. Among the noteworthy exploits are those of Rusty Baillie, Doug Scott, Spain's Gallego brothers, and the locals Howell and Allan. The best known route, pioneered in 1973 by Phil Snyder and T. Mathenge, is the one that ascends the Diamond Couloir, a sheer route of ice. Two years after that, the American climber Yvon Chouinard blazed a direct route up the final sheer stretch—a climb that soon acquired mythical standing throughout the world.

The best known adventure, however, befell three Italians. In 1943, Felice Benuzzi, Giovanni Balletto, and Vincenzo Barsotti escaped from the British POW camp at Nanyuki and reached the base of the mountain. They attempted, unsuccessfully, to climb Batian, and then went on to climb the easier—but still quite high, at 16,355 feet—Point Lenana. They finally made their way back to camp dying of starvation; there they were punished by their English captors for their escape attempt. But Benuzzi's account of their adventures —*No Picnic on Mount Kenya*—was to become one of the great classics of mountain literature.

Umberto woke me: "Hurry! Get up! You can see Mount Kenya." I jumped out of my cot and put on my shoes. "If you don't hurry, it'll be covered in clouds." "How's it look?" "Not bad. It's sort of like Monviso, but bigger. Get moving!" I got out, I slopped some distance through the mud, and there it was, framed between two black huts. I was stunned. I never expected it to be so beautiful. Silvery, wreathed in clouds, sharp, stark, inset in ice that glittered with a bluish cast, there it was, Mount Kenya, the second tallest mountain in Africa, the first 5,000-meter peak that I had ever laid eyes on—indomitable.

Felice Benuzzi

It was seven in the morning when we left this large ledge and climbed the accessible rocks that led from the northeast ridge to Point Lenana. We were incredibly tired, and the verglas on the rocks was causing a lot of problems, but the higher we climbed, the clearer the sky became. On our right the immense northeast wall of Nelion glowed with a yellow so luminous that it helped us to forget all our fatigue. Even today, if I close my eyes and try to summon up that vision, I see that chrome yellow—rich, lively— a yellow like that found on the old houses of Rome in the fall, before sunset tinges them with vermillion.

Felice Benuzzi

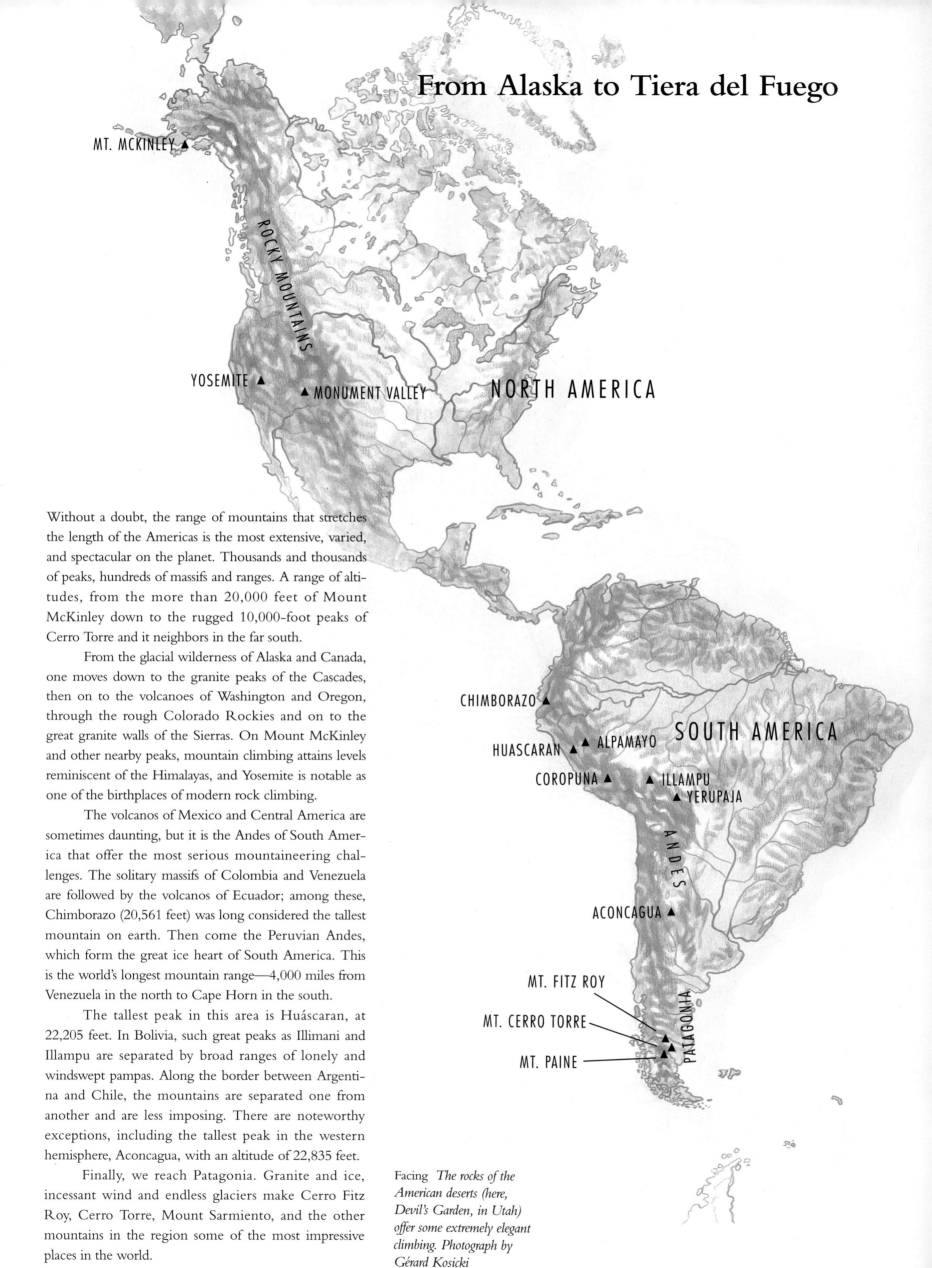

From Alaska to Tiera del Fuego

MT. MCKINLEY ▲

ROCKY MOUNTAINS

YOSEMITE ▲

▲ MONUMENT VALLEY

NORTH AMERICA

CHIMBORAZO ▲

HUASCARAN ▲ ▲ ALPAMAYO

SOUTH AMERICA

COROPUNA ▲ ▲ ILLAMPU

▲ YERUPAJA

ANDES

ACONCAGUA ▲

MT. FITZ ROY

MT. CERRO TORRE

MT. PAINE

PATAGONIA

Without a doubt, the range of mountains that stretches the length of the Americas is the most extensive, varied, and spectacular on the planet. Thousands and thousands of peaks, hundreds of massifs and ranges. A range of altitudes, from the more than 20,000 feet of Mount McKinley down to the rugged 10,000-foot peaks of Cerro Torre and it neighbors in the far south.

From the glacial wilderness of Alaska and Canada, one moves down to the granite peaks of the Cascades, then on to the volcanoes of Washington and Oregon, through the rough Colorado Rockies and on to the great granite walls of the Sierras. On Mount McKinley and other nearby peaks, mountain climbing attains levels reminiscent of the Himalayas, and Yosemite is notable as one of the birthplaces of modern rock climbing.

The volcanos of Mexico and Central America are sometimes daunting, but it is the Andes of South America that offer the most serious mountaineering challenges. The solitary massifs of Colombia and Venezuela are followed by the volcanos of Ecuador; among these, Chimborazo (20,561 feet) was long considered the tallest mountain on earth. Then come the Peruvian Andes, which form the great ice heart of South America. This is the world's longest mountain range—4,000 miles from Venezuela in the north to Cape Horn in the south.

The tallest peak in this area is Huáscaran, at 22,205 feet. In Bolivia, such great peaks as Illimani and Illampu are separated by broad ranges of lonely and windswept pampas. Along the border between Argentina and Chile, the mountains are separated one from another and are less imposing. There are noteworthy exceptions, including the tallest peak in the western hemisphere, Aconcagua, with an altitude of 22,835 feet.

Finally, we reach Patagonia. Granite and ice, incessant wind and endless glaciers make Cerro Fitz Roy, Cerro Torre, Mount Sarmiento, and the other mountains in the region some of the most impressive places in the world.

Facing *The rocks of the American deserts (here, Devil's Garden, in Utah) offer some extremely elegant climbing. Photograph by Gérard Kosicki*

Mount McKinley
Treacherous Jaws of Ice

"The mountains of Alaska are not the tallest in the world the great summits of the Himalayas tower a good thousand or two thousand meters above them. But in the Himalayas, the snowline is at five or six thousand meters. Around Mount McKinley, the entire region is blanketed by perennial snow and ice." With these words, Claude F. Kusk described the scene more than eighty years ago, as the first expedition set out to scale the tallest mountain in North America. Kusk was certainly correct. In the state that Czar Alexander II sold to the United States in 1867, the great mountain chains form one of the most inhospitable and savage expanses of wilderness in the world.

The climate at the top of McKinley is among the harshest in the world, outside the polar regions. Much the same may be said for Mount Deborah, Mount Saint Lhas, and Mount Logan—for all of the major peaks in Canada's British Columbia and in Alaska, caught between the gales of the Pacific and the storms of the Arctic. Mount McKinley (which was called *Denali* by the Athapaskan Indians) was introduced to mountain climbing during the Klondike gold rush of the turn of this century. The race for the peak of Mount McKinley was just dramatic enough to match this context.

In 1906, the first expedition to try to scale the peak was led by Frederick A. Cook. The nine weeks it took the team to reach the base of the mountain, on foot and by canoe, give a first indication of the scale of the challenge. Then came glaciers, the lower slopes of the mountain itself, and the pitfalls of high altitude. On his return, Cook wrote in *Harper's Monthly* that he had reached the peak. The leader of the expedition had been to the Arctic four times, and at first no one questioned his word. Then doubt began to spread. Four years later, Belmore Brown and Herschel Parker discovered, at a distance of twenty miles from McKinley, the mountain top where Cook took his "victory photograph." This "peak" was only about 6,500 feet tall, Thus 14,000 feet short of the true peak. Cook became a victim of his own deceit. The discovery of his trickery concerning Mount McKinley undercut the veracity of his claim to have reached the North Pole several weeks prior to Robert F. Peary. "How ironic it would be if the fraud of Mount McKinley denied glory to the first man to reach the North Pole!" wrote Chris Jones in 1976, in his book *Climbing North America*.

There was no shortage of new challengers ready to climb the mountain. In 1910, the Sourdoughs, a group of miners from Fairbanks led by Tom Lloyd, climbed the north peak of McKinley, slightly lower than the south peak. In 1912, Belmore Brown returned, and came within 160 feet (in vertical distance) of the peak. The following year, Hudson Stuck, Walter Harper, Harry Karstens, and Robert Tatum reached the long sought peak, at 20,320 feet. This was an remarkable achievement for a team that was without modern equipment and almost totally ignorant of advanced mountain climbing techniques.

Modern mountaineering came to Mount McKinley in 1961, when Dan Sheldon, the "ice pilot," landed a plane at the foot of the south wall with six climbers from Lecco, in Italy. The expedition was led by Riccardo Cassin, 52, legendary conqueror of the Grandes Jorasses, Piz Badile, and the Tre Cime. With him were Luigi Airoldi, Gigi Alippi, Jack Canali, Romano Perego, and Annibale Zucchi. None spoke a word of English, and they had all crossed the ocean for the first time. The route they followed stuck to a very distinct spur, the most clearly defined on the slope. On 13 July, Zucchi and Perego conquered the most difficult part, and prepared Camp III at 17,000 feet. Then the weather worsened. An opportunity came on July 19, and the old fox Cassin took full advantage. At eleven o'clock, in the clear arctic night, the group had reached the peak. All of them were chilled, and many had symptoms of frostbite. On their way down, in the gale, Canali discovered that his hands and feet were now seriously frozen. The Italian climbers were equipped for the Alps but Mount McKinley demanded Antarctic or Everest standards of the kind of preparation.

Back in Europe, Cassin's climb was just one more instance of his bravura. But in Alaska, it inaugurated a more authentic school of climbing. A number of other routes were opened, the west spur (Davidson, Genet, and Johnston, 1977), the direct route up the south slope (Eberl, Laba, Siedman, and Thompson, 1977), and the seemingly endless northeast "Ridge of No Return," soloed by Renato Casarotto 1984.

Today, air taxis shuttle between Talkeetna and the glacier. Five hundred climb the peak each year, and over 50,000 visit the park. Yet in May 1992, a terrible storm killed eleven climbers. Climbing in Alaska continues, however with extremely difficult routes being inaugurated such as Deprivation which Marc Twight and Scott Backes opened in the summer of '94 on the North Spur of Mount Hunter.

Silently acknowledging the energy-sapping properties of a hollow debate, we backed away from the confrontation, fixing our glassy stares on the snow ahead as we resumed our task. When we emerged from the steep slope onto the summit plateau, the pure magic of the mountain took over. The constant metamorphosis of scenery, light, and clouds had suddenly crystallized into a 360-degree panorama of mountain tops and cotton-candy cloud floor. Amazingly, the bitter wind died completely.

We floated up the final 300 feet of the summit wedge through thick, lingering alpenglow and, at 11 P.M., topped out just as the sun was beginning to lose its grip on the edge of the world. A deep-freeze breeze oozed up from the dark South Face like liquid nitrogen. Our faces and head gear were covered in hoar-frost in the still minus-30°F air. The summit was a desktop-sized parking lot of bamboo wands and shredded flags, towering over an empty Japanese Asahi beer can. Everything was right in the world tonight.

Pat Morrow

A climber works up a long snow ridge on the slopes of Mount McKinley. Photograph by Pat Morrow/First Light

Mount McKinley is a magnet for climbers. Like Mount Everest, it lures large numbers of unsuspecting people onto its frozen slopes. The results can be fatal. Every year climbers get caught in storms on this big mountain and perish. Although there are several good technical routes on McKinley, most of the hundreds of climbers choose the well-trod west buttress route. Lulled into thinking they are safe because there are so many other climbers nearby, even experienced climbers let down their guard and are caught by altitude sickness or bad weather. If only climbers would show more respect for this mountain there would be far fewer incidents. My team, however, was very determined and well equipped. Up we trudged, in misty unsettled conditions, pondering the intelligence of our decisions. It was miserable going—one step, break through the crust of the deteriorating conditions, curse; another step, throbbing head, ten to fifteen breaths; another step . . .

Unburdened by a pack, Bernhard surged ahead on the wind-packed sections, the rope between us always taut.

"Why don't you put some of that extra energy into nicking steps for me?" I yelled resentfully, my anger rising in a crescendo. I stabbed my way up to him, stiff-legged, two mongrels glowering at each other. Two extremely tired mongrels.

Three weeks' worth of pent-up emotions from living in such close quarters had suddenly turned septic. Close friends were about to ruin their summit chances and mess up the scenery by planting ice axes in each other's chest.

Pat Morrow

Normal expeditions take a month to climb the peak. What made us think we could do it so quickly? Although we were more fit than most men in their mid-thirties, we were no more so than the thousands of men, women, and children who can run twenty-six mile marathons in less than three hours. At 19,000 feet two small figures approached from below as we lay sprawled in the snow resting, all dignity abandoned. The two men stopped and eyed the obviously unfit and out-of-place climbers at their feet, and one of them remarked, "Anyone who needs a rope up here doesn't belong on this mountain!" The British accent identified him as one of the men whose sleep we had interrupted at 17,300 feet. When we introduced ourselves, their attitude became friendlier. The Britisher, Nigel Gifford, had been on expeditions to Everest and Nuptse and was planning to look me up as a climbing partner in California. His companion, John Purdue, was a Canadian. Nigel's comment about the rope made Ned and I realize that we could do without the extra weight, so

we left both rope and packs lying in the snow when we again set off. All four of us started out together, but because of Nigel and John's rest and acclimatization, Ned and I quickly were left behind. I soon began to feel like a zombie, while Ned's nausea disappeared. Our roles were being reversed, and Ned was not the stronger, but our cooperative efforts kept us going.

As we neared 20,000 feet, we watched Nigel and John reach the summit, turn around, and start back down. When they stopped only a hundred feet below the top and didn't move for a long time, we wondered if something was wrong. We reached them half an hour later and found them sitting on a platform they had stamped into the steep slope, with their stove humming reassuringly in the still air. With the air of a proper British gentleman, Nigel inquired, "Would you like a cup of tea?"

Galen Rowell

In the space of a few minutes, the wind became very strong,
sweeping the slopes and raising great clouds of powdery snow. The
thermometer dropped sharply. It must have been fifty degrees
below zero, and the wind chill factor made it twice as cold. I real-
ized that I should stop, but I was anxious, and I continued. I
went on without even putting on my parka. At 10:30, I reached
the top of the South Buttress. But it was hell. The wind was
blowing so hard that I could barely stand up. I decided to open by
backpack and set up my tent. As the hours passed, I acquired the
mental clarity needed to evaluate the situation. The thought of the
days gone by throttled my stomach and oppressed me.

Renato Casarotto

Below   The team of the U.S. expedition to Mount McKinley in 1979 makes its way through a blizzard. Photograph by Galen Rowell

Yosemite
Walls of Granite

Yosemite Valley, 1869 . . . A young man, born in Scotland, spent the summer of his thirty-first year wandering through the forests, boulders, and waterfalls of what was to become the most famous valley in America. "I reached the peak at midday, after stopping along the way to study some trees," John Muir recalled later, after climbing Cathedral Peak. During those same years, "real" mountain climbing began to develop in the Alps, but Muir's concept of the mountains was different. He sought to wander through the wilderness not to conquer the mountains, but to gain a sense of harmony with them. This love of nature drove John Muir to fight to save the Sierra valleys, threatened by the construction of dams, the felling of trees, and the cutting of roads. In 1890, Yosemite National Park was established, thanks in large part to his efforts.

Summer of 1975 . . . "An alarm sounds at 2:00 A.M. Three bodies arise quickly. They dress a la Jimi Hendrix, and sit to a breakfast of omelettes and beans." In the seventies, Yosemite had become one of the most important locations for mountain climbing in the world. On the day described here, Jim Bridwell, John Long, and Bill Westbay, were attempting to be the first team to climb the Nose in just one day. The Nose was the most classic way up El Capitan, the tallest wall in the valley. Eighteen years earlier, the first to climb this route, Warren Harding, took seventeen days of actual climbing and 125 bolts.

To continue with Bill Westbay's description of the day: "We take off at 4:00 A.M., on the initial pitches rehearsed a few days before, but this time under the light of headlamps." The first third of the climb was made with Long in the lead, followed by Westbay as the leader in the middle third, while Bridwell had to lead through the difficult fissures in the top third. "At 7:00 P.M., three weary bodies stand of the summit of El Cap, and begin an epic descent."

In Europe, for many decades, little or nothing was known about climbing in California. Carved out by a glacier millions of years ago, the valley where the Merced River runs is surrounded by walls that are the body of the surrounding highlands. Half Dome, on the other hand, is a real mountain; it was first climbed in 1875 and was soon equipped with cables. Certainly, the finest spires, such as Lost Arrow and the Cathedral Spires—which stand opposite El Capitan—are every bit as challenging and attractive as the Aiguilles in Chamonix or the towers of the Dolomites. The normal route up El Capitan is nothing more than a trail among the rocks, but the nearly 3,300-foot wall is one of the most daunting in the world. The first exploits took place in 1933 on the Higher Cathedral Spire (Eichorn, Leonard, and Robinson), and continued the following year on the nearby and more difficult Lower Cathedral Spire (the same three climbers).

In the postwar period, John Salathé was the first to climb the Lost Arrow, the most handsome spire in the valley, and the southwest wall of Half Dome, developing approaches and equipment suited to the adamantine granite of Yosemite. Steel pitons were the first step toward an entirely American technology. During the fifties, Yosemite began to be frequented by other names destined for glory—Allen Steck, Royal Robbins, and Yvon Chouinard. In the spring of 1957, along with Jerry Gallwas and Mike Sherrick, Robbins climbed the northwest face of Half Dome, the first episode in the history of big wall climbing, and the first Grade VI climb in the United States. Even more monumental exploits were near at hand—during the Fourth of July weekend Warren Harding, Bill Fuerer, and Mike Powell began the assault on the Nose. Unsuccessful attempts, climbs and descents on fixed ropes, and disputes with park rangers who looked on the enterprise with a jaundiced eye were the keynotes of the following months. Fuerer and Powell gave up the effort. The following year, Harding finally climbed onto the peak, together with Wayne Merry.

In the sixties and seventies, the wall was scaled along a number of routes, and the valley was crowded with climbers. The routes were in full exposure, and entailed extremely dangerous pitches (the A5 "guarantees" that a climber will fall at least one hundred feet), with climbers dangling at crazy angles or sleeping in hammocks suspended over the void. The names assigned to the routes in the seventies were emblematic of the time—Mescalito, Tangerine Trip, Sea of Dreams, and Excalibur. So was a remarkable and admirable new school of climbing. When the first European climbers arrived in Yosemite, they were often terrorized by the level of physical stamina and mental and technical preparation required by this new school. While in the Alps, climbers still made extensive use of slings, free-climbing was born in Yosemite, where the use of pitons was a crime. The Californian school developed "clean climbing" as well, where it was forbidden to leave anything behind on the wall. These philosophies, the heritage of John Muir, had a powerful influence on European climbing in the eighties.

The Desert Spires of America
Architecture in Stone

Left *Luisa Jovine is shown working her way up the slabs of Red Rocks in Nevada. Photograph by Heinz Mariacher*

Facing *A crucial phase in the ascent of Moses Tower, rearing up into the skies over Utah. Photograph by Heinz Mariacher*

Pumas and coyotes, sand storms, endless roads, John Wayne, and Geronimo. Very few places in the world have been described in film and photographs like the American southwest, and few places on the planet are so rich in spectacular wilderness areas. In the Grand Canyon, rafting and hiking take on a flavor of adventure unequalled anywhere else. At Canyon de Chelly and Mesa Verde, the charm of nature joins with the allure of history and archeology.

Today, climbers from around the world aspire to travel to the rocks of Joshua Tree, Hueco Tanks, Windy Point, and the City of Rocks in New Mexico. Rock climbing, however, is nothing new here. A symbol of the burgeoning field of mountain climbing in the southwest is Ship Rock, an imposing volcanic tower in the northwestern corner of New Mexico. It is more than 7,000 feet tall, and can be seen from the Old Spanish Trail. The Navajo call it *Tsa-Beh-Tai*, the "Rock with Wings."

The first team to try scaling Ship Rock came from Colorado. Robert Ormes was the leader of the group, and with him were Gordon Williams, Mel Griffiths, and Bill House. House later gave his name to the most difficult and challenging section of the Abruzzi Spur on K2. On Ship Rock, his role was to halt a plunge into the void by Ormes; in the end, Ormes was dangling from just one piton. Later, Robert Ormes wrote an article for an evening paper about the experience. The headline read: "A Piece of Bent Iron." Ormes did not return to Ship Rock. In 1939, a team from California finally reached the peak, and three decades later, in 1970, the great climber from Yosemite, Chuck Pratt, was to describe the mountain as "an image out of Genesis . . . which imposes silence."

In 1955, Mark Powell, Jerry Gallwas, and Jim Wilson attempted to climb the sandstone spires in Arizona's Canyon de Chelly. First they scaled Spider Rock, then Cleopatra's Needle, and lastly the slender Totem Pole, some 350 feet tall—so spindly that, Chris Jones wrote, "the very thought of its existence seems absurd." Other remarkable adventures have taken place in Utah. In 1961, Layton Kor, Fred Beckey, Harvey Carter, and Huntley Ingalls climbed the Titan, a tower more than 650 feet tall.

In the seventies, challenging climbs requiring lengthy treks and exposure to vile weather conditions were pioneered on a number of rocky structures in the Grand Canyon. Today, lower peaks are receiving the

greatest attention. The modern trend toward safety-oriented climbing clashes with the severe ethics of clean climbing, which barely accepts pitons, much less bolts; at times, the strict regulations of national parks come into play as well. A great many peaks, moreover, are off limits in keeping with the wishes of Indian tribes. After all, before they became recreational facilities for climbers, these stone structures in the desert were sacred monuments to the Hopi, the Navajo, and the Apache Indians.

When we reached the meadows of San Bonaventura de Miera, we sensed the mystery of a land that spoke of eternity. The Moses Tower was crushing us. We were overwhelmed by this desert monster 650 feet tall, with great sheer drops on all sides. There were a number of different routes, but none of them seemed possible. We did not even make a try, but spent two days in its shadow, on the Zeus Tower, only half as high. Climbing on crumbly sandstone is a test of perseverance, with an extremely fitful wind that makes every action more difficult and eliminates any chance we had of talking to each other. The temperatures are always wrong—it is either biting cold or stifling hot. Every day is a distillation of the mountain climbing experience of an entire life.

Fred Beckey

Alpamayo
The Mountain of Mountains

Which is the finest ice wall in the world? Climbers who spend a lot of time in the Alps may think of the Lyskamm or the Brenva, while those who have been to the Himalayas might suggest the east wall of Everest or the north wall of Annapurna. Alpamayo, however, seduces one at first sight. All that's needed is a glance at a photograph of this Andean mountain to understand that there simply could not be a better looking wall. Curlicues, arabesques, and cannelures of ice make this 19,600-foot peak a cult object for mountain climbers around the world.

The greatest concentration of handsome, tall, savage, and difficult peaks is, without a doubt, in the Peruvian Andes, where all of the best known mountains are in the Cordillera Blanca, which extend for about 120 miles north of Lima, and in the Cordillera Huayhuash. Mountain climbing is a venerable art on these ice ridges. In 1908, the lower, north peak of Huascarán was conquered. Three years after that, in 1911, the American archeologist, Hiram Bingham, who discovered Machu Picchu in the same year, first climbed the 21,702-foot peak of Coropuna. In 1932, an Austro-German expedition led by Paul Borchers climbed nearly all the major peaks in this area.

After World War II, these mountains all became classics. The reasons are quite evident—here, in locations that could easily be reached from Europe and North America, it was possible to climb world-class mountains without the expense, the bureaucracy, and the long approaches of the Himalayas. All, or almost all, of the major names left their mark here. Walter Bonatti and Andrea Oggioni climbed the Rondoy, in 1963; Reinhold Messner climbed the Yerupajá; Riccardo Cassin led an expedition up the Jirishanca, a needle whose name means "Hummingbird's Beak" in the language of the Quechua Indians; and Renato Casarotto climbed the nightmarish wall of South Huascarán. René Desmaison, Lionel Terray, Giancarlo Grassi, and Toni Egger all boast achievements of like stature.

Among all of the climbs, the Ragni Route from Lecco up the southwest wall of Alpamayo—its name has nothing to do with the Alps, and means "Muddy River" in Quechua—first blazed in 1975, became the best known in the Andes. Every summer, dozens of teams make the same climb, which is actually not terribly difficult. Thanks to the new equipment for ice climbing, it has now become accessible to a great many climbers.

After a long hike, we finally reached the foot of Alpamayo, the mountain of mountains, a thousand meters (3,280 feet) taller than the highest Alpine summit. The light was so strong that our eyes stung, despite our sunglasses. A glittering pyramid of ice soaring toward the heavens. And we wanted to climb up there! A labyrinth of ice towers, crevasses, and snow bridges lay in our path . . . Toward evening the clouds scattered, and the mountains appeared in all their splendor, wrapped in the light of sunset. The wall was so steep that the snow broke away at the slightest vibration, and we enjoyed a refreshing shower of snow. After hours of tough climbing on the ice we finally reached the ridge. We could hear the wind whistle, the weather had darkened, the clouds were gathering in a dark layer that promised nothing good. The spirit of the group became as downcast as the weather was overcast; there was no glee when we reached the summit.

Albert Gruber

Cerro Torre and Cerro Fitz Roy
Ferocious Summits of Patagonia

North wall of Cerro Torre, February 1, 1959 . . . The most handsome and savage mountain in the Andes is trying to destroy the two men who, twenty-four hours previous, first walked on its summit. On the descent, the men are fighting for their lives. Cesare Maestri, of Trento, was the "Spider of the Dolomites," one of the most famous climbers of all time. His fellow-climber, Toni Egger, from Lienz in Austria, was equally distinguished. His name is linked to the conquest of Jirishanca, at 20,099 feet, the icy "Matterhorn of the Andes." The climb up Cerro Torre was a three-day adventure on vertical granite walls, with sheer plunges of flaking sheets of ice, interspersed with fatiguing crevasses. Finally, they gained the summit, but with victory came the deadly wind that comes off the Pacific.

"A titanic blow . . . an irresistible force . . . cataclysmic," Maestri was to write upon his return. As they descended, after getting past the Colle della Conquista, the spires of rock standing before Cerro Torre protected the climbers from the roughest gales of wind. It was evening. Maestri wanted to call a halt there, camp on the face of Cerro Torre, and wait until dawn to continue down the nearly 1,000 feet of rope they had attached on the way up. That, however, would take them down to the glacier where Cesarino Fava was waiting for them, and Egger wanted to continue. Maestri lowered Egger for about 1,000 feet, but then came the disaster. "There was a strange noise, a stronger gale of wind," recalls Maestri, and then came the avalanche. "Suddenly, an immense wall of snow rushed out of the fog."

When it was all over, the end of the rope dangled lazily in the wind. Further down, fallen snow had covered the glacier. Maestri was all alone. Reaching the bottom took hours, and at the end, the last rappel unraveled from its pitons. Maestri fell until he hit the soft snow, which saved his life. Fava finally found him, half-buried and stunned, on the evening of February 3. The two climbers left, down toward the moraine, then on to Laguna Torre, Buenos Aires, and Europe. But they did not leave Cerro Torre entirely behind them, as we shall see.

At 10,262 feet, Cerro Torre is certainly not the tallest mountain in Patagonia. A few miles east, Cerro Torre's twin, Cerro Fitz Roy, is nearly 1,000 feet taller. Further north, the Cerro San Lorenzo soars to 12,159 feet, while the San Valentin is more than 13,000 feet. But none of these has the daunting reddish vertical walls of Cerro Torre. In Patagonia, altitude is of relative impor-

tance. When the gales blow off the Pacific, with the super chill that they acquire over the huge glacier, Hielo Continental, one is risking one's life even at sea level. For mountaineering in Patagonia, wind is the dominant factor, and that wind can keep climbers from moving for weeks at a time. "A two-month stay in a refrigerator, from which we emerged every day to go toss a hundred-mark note in the toilet," is how the German mountain climber Reinhard Karl—who climbed Cerro Fitz Roy in 1982—recalled an unfortunate expedition to Patagonia. Visitors to this desolate land have been captivated by precisely these elements—the brutal climate, the savage appearance, and the romantic solitude.

Among the most famous of those visitors were the Italian explorer Alberto Maria De Agostini and the late Bruce Chatwin, the author of *In Patagonia*, and, of course, Cesare Maestri. The Trentine climber first learned about Cerro Torre in the southern summer of 1957-1958, when there were two Italian expeditions operating in the area. Walter Bonatti and Carlo Mauri, with an expedition of Lombard climbers, attempted to scale it from the west; they reached a saddle that they called the Col of Hope. Maestri, on the other hand, climbing with an expedition from Trento, observed the mountain from the east, decided that it was not feasible, and then set out for other objectives. He returned the year after, and conquest and tragedy ensued, as described above.

Later, the story of Cerro Torre began to twist and warp into a mystery. A British expedition (Mick Burke, Pete Crew, Martin Boysen, and Dougal Haston) attempted to climb Cerro Torre in 1967-1968 and failed. They were followed by a team of Japanese and Spanish climbers. In 1969 a group from Lecco called the *Ragni*, or "Spiders," was also unsuccessful.

On their return, an infamous accusation began to circulate. Had Maestri and Egger ever really climbed Cerro Torre? Maestri was not the sort of man to get bogged down in discussions or to try to reconstruct a detailed map of the route he took. He just got angry, and returned to Cerro Torre in 1970, this time quite determined to prove his superiority over the mountain. He brought with him—besides a group of friends from Trento—an Atlas Copco compressor that he used to drive bolts. At the base of the ice overhangs at the summit, Maestri stopped. He descended. And there he left the compressor, where it still hangs—a lightning rod for debates that still rage in the world of international mountain climbing.

Below *A team of climbers from Trento, Italy, ascends the last stretch of Cerro Torre, within sight of the ice overhang at the peak. This route makes use of bolts driven by Cesare Maestri in 1970. Photograph by Maurizio Giarolli/Dalpez Archives*

Facing *A raging blizzard makes the climb down from the peak of Cerro Torre even tougher during the first winter expedition, made in 1985 by Paolo Caruso, Maurizio Giarolli, Andrea Sarchi, and Erano Salvaterra. Photograph by Maurizio Giarolli/Dalpez Archives*

The greatest indignation seethed among the English on the pages of the respected magazine *Mountain*, which levelled accusations at the Italian climbers. In the movie, *The Cerro Torre Enigma*, director Leo Dickinson wondered openly whether the mountain had ever been scaled. In 1974, when the Ragni, led by Casimiro Ferran, reached the peak from the west side, *Mountain* ran a headline reading: "Cerro Torre Climbed," implicitly stating that this was the first time. The next year, the glacier gave up the remains of Egger, but without the camera that should have contained photographs of the peak. Case closed? Not really, to judge from the film *Cry of Stone* by Werner Herzog, 1991, which investigated the mystery of Cerro Torre for millions of viewers around the world.

Ever since the end of the seventies, Cerro Torre

has been climbed repeatedly, setting aside the world of disputes. In 1979, Jim Bridwell, the climber from Yosemite, climbed the Via del Compressore together with Steve Brewer. In order to climb the last stretch, from the compressor to the ice, which had in the meanwhile retracted, Bridwell and Brewer had to rely on all of their experience and all of their sklll. On the way down, tragedy was once again narrowly averted. Then a new series of triumphs ensued. In 1983, the climbers Maurizio Giarolli and Ermanno Salvaterra, from Trento, once again made the same climb, and improved the pitons on the last stretch. Two years later, the same two climbers returned with Paolo Caruso and Andrea Sarchi to make the first winter climb. In 1986, a very accomplished Yugoslavian expedition climbed the east wall, blazing a new route with levels of difficulty ranging up to Grade VIII.

That same year the Argentineans Sebastian de la Cruz, Gabriel Ruiz and Eduardo Brenner completed the first winter ascent of the Fitz Roy. Another remarkable exploit on this mountain was that of the Swiss climber Kaspar Ochsner and the Czech Michal Pitelka who scaled the extremely compact East Pillar in 1991. On Cerro Torre, the attention of the best climbers was instead concentrated on the sheer South Face, over 4,900 feet high and dominating the Torre glacier. The first to climb the face in 1988 were the Slovenians Janez Jeglic and Silvo Karo. An even more difficult route was opened in the winter of 1995 by the Italians Ermanno Salvaterra, Piergiorgio Vidi and Roberto Manni.

Today, the standard route up Cerro Torre is largely equipped with fixed ropes. The extremely sheer walls, however, the violent gales, and the avalanches will prevent this mountain from ever becoming a popular or fashionable climb.

On Cerro Fitz Roy, on the Torres del Paine, and on many other mountains of the region, great ascents were made. The peaks surrounding Cerro Torre were climbed, one after the other These were the Aguja Bifida, the Cerro Standhardt, and El Mocho. The most savage and difficult peak was scaled in 1976 by an AngloAmerican team consisting of John Bragg, John Donini and Jay Wilson. They named this peak Torre Egger, in commemoration of the Austrian climber who died on Cerro Torre. Solidarity among climbers is greater than rivalry; just as blood is thicker than water.

We climbed into our tent and waited for the weather to improve. My sleeping bag was just a block of cement by this point; I looked at it and comforted myself by dreaming of the warmth it would be giving me if it only had been dry. We faced only the 650 feet of the final wall, completely blanketed by six or seven inches of ice and snow. It was necessary to cut a vertical ditch to uncover the bolts that Maestri had set fifteen years before. Hanging on my sling, I had to dig out a square meter or so of ice with my ice axe; it came away in blocks and fell straight onto the heads of my friends down below. Then we all reached the top. The sun was setting over the Hielo Continental with metallic highlights, the Antarctic chill was falling on us like a weight. The descent was going to be long and difficult. And night was approaching rapidly.

Andrea Sarchi

Patagonia—one of those names that had set me daydreaming as a child: adventures, shipwrecks, and all the things a child dreams of after reading too many adventure stories. Certainly, I could not imagine then that one day I would find in Patagonia one of the most interesting playing fields a mountain climber could hope for.

Maurizio Giarolli

Oceania and Antarctica
Solitary Mountains of Ice

"Hours and hours of flying over unclimbed and nameless peaks, over walls as vast as the north face of the Eiger," is how the great mountain climber, Chris Bonington, described the view during a flight from the British base of Rothera to the base of the Vinson Massif, the tallest peak in Antarctica. Standing 16,860 feet tall, this mountain demands the commitment that was required to scale Everest or any other 8,000-meter peak—and perhaps even more, given the raging winds, the chill that plunges to fifty degrees below zero Celsius, and the stark, absolute isolation.

The first to climb Vinson, in 1966, was a team from the American Alpine Club led by Nicholas B. Clinch. Today, an attempt is made to scale the peak each year. Vinson, however, is not the only peak in Antarctica. Interminable ranges, colossal walls, enormous and hazardous glaciers poke up all over the lunar landscape of the frozen continent, and especially on the Antarctic Peninsula, in the Sentinel Range and the Admiralty Range.

And Antarctica is not the only land "down under" in the final and fitting chapter to this book. Among all the mountains in the southern hemisphere, the best known are New Zealand's Southern Alps — spectacular peaks, savage, raked by merciless winds, and laced with ice arabesques. Mount Cook, 12,349 feet tall, is certainly tougher than its "height equivalent" in the Alps or the Rockies. In Australia, the jagged peaks of Mount Arapiles and other, smaller mountains attract climbers from all over the world at all times of the year.

The real mountains, however, are unquestionably minor—Kosciusko, 7,310 feet tall, is the highest peak in Australia. To the north, the Irian Jaya, a range which covers the western, Indonesian half of New Guinea, features the Carstencz Pyramid, an unsettling mountain that is perennially wrapped in clouds, one of the most isolated and impressive peaks in the world. The islands complete the picture. Dense forests cluster around the modest peaks of Tasmania, and the winds of the Roaring Forties batter the Ball Pyramid, an 1,844-foot-tall sea stack that has been the fond goal of generations of Australian climbers. Further south, at the gates of Antarctica, the island of South Georgia holds savage peaks covered with ice. The Earth's Deep South has a great many adventures in store.

Facing The American climber Greg Mortimer climbs near the summit of the Vinson Massif, the highest mountain in Antarctica. In the background are the silhouettes of the Ellsworth Mountains. Photograph by Colin Monteath/Hedgehog House

Mount Cook
Mountain Climbing Down Under

"They are prodigious in height . . . the peaks and most of the valleys are covered with snow." With these words, in 1770, Captain James Cook—the great explorer of the oceans and continents "hidden" in the Earth's southern hemisphere—described the Southern Alps, the huge mountains of New Zealand. Cook observed the mountains from the sea, and was amazed by their appearance and glaciers, even from dozens of miles away. Ninety years later, when the colonization of the southern continent was well underway, one of the first whites to live in the area, Samuel Butler, wrote about the mountains again. "I am wasting time observing a mountain that can be of no possible use for sheep . . . At any rate, I think that no human being can ever reach those peaks." Butler was an English novelist and painter, well known for his imaginative novel, *Erewhon*, but he was wrong about the mountains of New Zealand.

Before the nineteenth century ended, the highest peaks of the Southern Alps had all been scaled. The tallest one (12,349 feet) was named after Captain Cook. A local team climbed it, in an impulse of regional pride, before the English climber, Edward Fitz Gerald, and the guide from Monte Rosa, Matthias Zurbriggen, could beat them to it. Shortly thereafter, however, Zurbriggen led his client up the difficult slopes of Mounts Sefton, Sealy, Haidinger, and Tasman; after that Zurbriggen climbed Mount Cook solo. The route he used, up the northeast ridge, is now considered to be the normal route. Isolated, remote, and populated by more sheep than human beings, the two main islands of New Zealand caught the attention of European climbers quite some time ago. Despite that, mountain climbing "down under" remained relatively unimportant in Europe until after World War II. Suddenly, in June 1953, the world of climbing gained a new respect for the mountains of New Zealand. Sir Edmund Hillary, the first man—with the Sherpa Tenzing Norgay—to reach the 29,028-foot summit of Mount Everest, was from New Zealand. Another New Zealander, George Lowe, was one of the most distinguished climbers during that expedition.

"I was not the strongest mountain climber in technical terms. But I was in good training and I had blazed a number of new routes on Cook, Tasman, and La Perouse. These were truly savage mountains, and before starting to climb you had to walk days and days with a huge backpack." That is how Edmund Hillary described mountain climbing in New Zealand to this writer several years ago. It was no accident that when Hillary first came to Europe he immediately felt at home amidst the towering walls, snow ridges, and huge open spaces of the Bernese Oberland, with their interminable approaches.

On Mount Cook, by far the most handsome and impressive mountain in the range, Hillary and Harry Ayres blazed a route up the difficult south ridge-a respectable achievement had it been on an equivalent mountain in the Alps. Later, the great problem of the massif became the Caroline Face, the southwest ice wall of Mount Cook, which rose 7,544 feet. There are those who compare it to the north wall of the Eiger. In 1970, this wall was scaled successfully and uneventfully for the first time, by the New Zealanders Pete Gough and John Glasgow, marking a major step forward in mountain climbing in New Zealand. Having scaled the Carstenz Pyramid in 1986, the Canadian climber and photographer Pat Morrow became the first Alpinist to have reached the highest peaks of all seven continents.

Perhaps the greatest surprise for visitors to the Southern Alps is the climate. At these latitudes, the earth is basically an almost uninterrupted belt of oceans swept by violent winds. All of the mountains in this region—the Southern Alps, the ranges of Patagonia, and mountains on the islands around Antarctica—are subject to sudden hurricanes, massive rainfall, and unheralded changes in the weather. Towards Westland, the narrow coastal strip that separates the Southern Alps from the open Pacific and which receives the brunt of the weather, New Zealand's alpine range descends almost all the way to the ocean in spectacular steps of ice. The three million inhabitants of New Zealand constitute one of the greatest nations of nature-, adventure-, mountain-, and ocean-lovers. Expeditions of Kiwis have climbed Everest a number of times, come very close to being the first to scale Makalu, and have been the first to scale Ama Dablam and Kangtega. Peter Hillary, the son of Sir Edmund, has also climbed Everest, and was the first to traverse all of the Himalayas on foot. Is this mere heredity? Or the love of adventure sinking deep roots into an entire people? Perhaps a little of both. But without their mountains, beginning with Mount Cook, the New Zealanders could never have attained the status they enjoy in the annals of world mountain climbing.

To climb on Mount Cook is indeed a privilege, with its elegant ice ridges and rock buttresses providing a variety of routes up the mountain from all sides. The classic ice arête of the east ridge is definitely one of the great climbs on Mount Cook. Soaring elegantly from the Grand Plateau to midway along the summit ridge, it is the most aesthetic line on the mountain. A midnight start from the high hut, catching a good freeze across the snowy expanses of the Plateau, halfway up the east ridge as the sun climbs above the foothills of the Southern Alps. The orange and mauve dawn sky, interrupted by the sharp silhouette of neighboring peaks, the cold ice of the ridge momentarily on fire while the Caroline and East Faces on either side of you radiate a temporary illusion of warmth.

Then to the wonderful summit ridge. Nearly two kilometers of convoluted cornices and wind-smoothed ridges, always so aware of the incredible exposure on both sides as you wander along unroped towards the High Peak of Mount Cook. In over six trips along this ridge, I've only once met another party . . . the emptiness of these fine peaks is a continual surprise to overseas climbers. Mount Cook is a unique and powerful mountain.

Nick Groves

Right *The south wall of Mount Cook rears up over a sea of clouds. Photograph by Dean Johnston/Hedgehog House*

Below *The light of dawn catches a team of climbers on the east ridge of Mount Cook, one of the most classic climbs in the Southern Alps of New Zealand. Photograph by Chris Bonington*

Above *A climber descends the east ridge of Mount Cook. Photograph by Mike Freeman/Hedgehog House*

PAGES 140–141
A view of the peak of Mount Hicks, beneath the north wall of Mount Cook, with the Tasman Sea visible in the distance. Photograph by Nick Groves/Hedgehog House

The Climbers and Photographers

STEFANO ARDITO

Born in 1954 in Rome, where he still lives, Ardito has been a mountain climber for some twenty years. He was a founding member of Mountain Wilderness, an international environmental association. His dedication to preserving the mountain environment led him to take part in Free K2, an expedition in 1990 to clean the mountain of the detritus left behind by climbing expeditions. Both journalist and photographer, he contributes regularly to a number of European periodicals devoted to nature and mountaineering. He is also the author of some thirty books about mountains and mountaineering and works regularly for Italian television.

PIERRE BEGHIN

Born in 1951 in Rotterdam, Béghin died in October 1992 on the great wall of Annapurna in Nepal. Considered to be one of the greatest French climbers, he was a professional mountaineer from 1970 until his death. He blazed some hundred new routes on the Alps, and he led more than ten expeditions in the Himalayas, scaling five 8,000s, including the Kanchenjunga, solo; he also blazed a direct route up the south wall of Makalu, also solo. In 1991, with Christophe Profit, he scaled K2 along the northwest ridge from Pakistan. As relics of his achievements, there are a number of articles published in newspapers and magazines and four books; from these, and from his work as a photographer, we can obtain some sense of his passion for the Himalayas.

ROBERT BÖSCH

Born in 1954 near Zurich, Bösch took a degree in geography and then went on to become a photographer and journalist. He has worked in the Himalayas, the Caucasus, the United States, South America, and Australia. He is familiar with the Alps and in 1990 took part in an expedition to the west ridge of Everest. Bösch has published articles and photographs in magazines and calendars, and is the author of the book, Bergsteigen—Verlockung des Ungewissen.

CHRIS BONINGTON

"Mr. Mountaineering," as he has been dubbed in his native Great Britain, was born in 1934 in Hampstead. Bonington attended the Royal Military Academy and went on to a military career, and from there to mountain climbing; he climbed in the Alps and was the first to scale the Freney Central Pillar along the south wall of Mont Blanc in 1961. He climbed the north face of the Eiger in 1962. Since then, his achievements have hardly gone unnoticed. Annapurna, Nuptse, Everest, K2, Ogre (a 23,900-foot peak in the Karakoram, not to be confused with the Eiger), Kongur, Shivling, Vinson Massif, and Menlungtse are among the peaks he has climbed. He has also explored the Blue Nile, and his adventuresome career includes other noteworthy chapters. Bonington has written numerous books and documentaries, has worked extensively as a lecturer, and is the chairman or a member of many important environmental groups.

MARK BUSCAIL

A French photographer, Buscail was born in Germany in 1951; he now lives in Les Deux Alpes. Beginning quite young, he has practiced a number of athletic activities, attaining remarkable levels of achievement. These activities (bobsledding, cross-country skiing, swimming, a parachute jump from Gasherbrum II at 26,360 feet) are an indication of the spirit of adventure that led him to explore the farthest-flung corners of the planet. He has traveled to mountains such as Manaslu and Kilimanjaro, as well as to India, the Middle East, and Tahiti.

TOMO CESEN

Born in Kranj, Slovenia, in 1959, Cesen is one of the most respected climbers in the world. He began to climb at the age of sixteen on the walls of the Julian Alps, and later on the massif of Mont Blanc. He has climbed about 200 new routes of considerable difficulty and is remarkably prepared in all sorts of areas—falaises, alpine walls in summer and winter, and mountains outside of Europe. Among the latter, most noteworthy are a new route up the south wall of Alpamayo, the north wall of Yalung Kang (a subsidiary summit of Kanchenjunga), and a solo ascent of Broad Peak, K2, the north wall of Jannu and, in 1990, the south face of Lhotse.

GREG CHILD

Born in Sydney, Australia in 1957, Child has lived in the United States since 1980. He is a mountain climber, photographer, journalist, and lecturer. His passion for mountaineering first began to develop in 1970. Since then he has climbed extensively in Yosemite Valley and made Himalayan expeditions up Lobsang Spire, Broad Peak, Gasherbrum IV, Makalu, Nameless Tower, Menlungtse, and K2. He works for the major Australian, Canadian, American, French, English, and Japanese magazines, and has lent his efforts to a number of books on the topic of mountain climbing.

JOHN CLEARE

Photographer, journalist, and lecturer, Cleare has published many books as well as newspaper and magazine articles. His travels have taken him from China to New Zealand, and from Ruwenzori to Cerro Fitz Roy. He has led sixteen minor expeditions on the mountains of the Himalayas and the Karakoram.

CHRIS CURRY

Curry is a New Zealander and a doctor; he has climbed Everest, Pik Kommunizm (Peak of Communism, formerly Stalin Peak, the highest in the former USSR), and Pumori.

MICHL DACHER

Born in 1933 in Germany, Dacher is an alpine guide and a ski instructor. His career as a climber began in 1949 on the Ammergauer mountains. Extremely active in the Alps, he climbed his first 8,000-meter peak, Yalung Kang (a subsidiary peak of Kanchenjunga), at the age of forty-two. The 8,000-meter peaks he has climbed in his career are Lhotse, K2, Shisha Pangma, Cho Oyu, Manaslu, Nanga Parbat, Broad Peak, Gasherbrum I and II, Makalu, and Everest. He has long been considered one of the finest climbers in the world, not only for his experience, but also because of his powerful physique.

ADRIANO DALPEZ

Born in 1945 in Malé, Italy, where he still lives, Dalpez is a photographer and freelance journalist. He contributes regularly to periodicals that feature mountaineering and the rural cultures of the mountains. He loves western Trento and frequents the Brenta group, as well as other groups in the Dolomites, where he climbs and photographs a number of classic routes. He has long been interested in the problems, the history, and the development of mountain climbing.

FABRIZIO DEFRANCESCO

As an alpine guide and climbing instructor at the Italian Police Alpine Academy in Moena, Defrancesco has been climbing full-time in the Alps since 1982. He has also climbed in Patagonia, scaling Cerro Astillado and the Paine Tower, as well as Cerro Fitz Roy twice; he has also climbed Aconcagua, Mount McKinley, and new routes in Canada and Alaska.

MICHEL FAUQUET

Nicknamed "Tchouky," Fauquet was born in Marseilles in 1962; he is an alpine guide as well as an instructor of skiing, parachuting, windsurfing, scuba diving, and spelunking. At the age of six, he was already climbing the Calanques outside his native Marseilles; at twelve, he began to climb seriously, in France, Italy, Spain, and in the U.S. He has scaled the Trango Towers, from which he parachuted, Makalu, and Khan Tengri, in the Tien Shan. In 1989, he took part in an unsuccessful expedition to climb Everest. He contributes to the leading European magazines in the field.

MIKE FREEMAN

Freeman is a heralded amateur climber from New Zealand.

PATRICK GABARROU

Born in 1951 in Normandy, Gabarrou studied philosophy at the Sorbonne, but he has since devoted himself to mountaineering, He has been an alpine guide for twenty years and has blazed countless routes on the Alps, especially on Mont Blanc, where his achievements are synonymous with great levels of difficulty on ice and mixed terrain. Outside of Europe, he has climbed Nanga Parbat, Nameless Tower, and Condoriri (Bolivia). He contributes to specialty periodicals around the world.

MAURIZIO GIAROLLI

Born in Cles, Italy, in 1958, Giarolli is a expert on Patagonia, especially Cerro Torre, Cerro Fitz Roy, and Cerro Poincenot. He has made successful climbs in the Himalayas, on Aconcagua, in Alaska, and in India, but he is fond of climbing in the Dolomites as well.

MAURIZIO GIORDANI

Born in 1959 in Rovereto, Giordani became an alpine guide in 1989, and he lectures widely on climbing and the environment. He began to explore the mountains and to climb at an early age. After consolidating his experience as a climber in the Alps on classic routes, he began to explore new routes. His climbs on the south wall of Marmolada are among the toughest and most spectacular in the Dolomites. In Patagonia, the Himalayas, and the Karakoram, he attained some important successes, relying on a rapid and precise style—although his main asset is determination.

DIDIER GIVOIS

Born in 1950 in France, Givois is an alpine guide, skiing, parachuting, and hang-gliding instructor, and a respected photographer. His photo essays on Tibet, Quebec, China, the Kamchatka peninsula, India, and Nepal are well known. He has done photography on parachuting, kayaking, canoeing, spelunking, and equitation.

ALESSANDRO GOGNA

Born in Genoa in 1946, Gogna as been an internationally known mountain climber for over twenty years. He opened 150 routes in the Alps and has made three expeditions outside of Europe; in 1979 he has been a member of an expedition to K2 led by Messner. He is the author of a dozen books and many monographs. Currently he is concentrating on the field of ecologically correct use of the mountains.

NICK GROVES

An English climber who lives in New Zealand, Groves is a member of the rescue squad in the National Park of Mount Cook. He has made a number of successful climbs in India and in the Karakoram.

ALBERT GRUBER

Born in Bressanone, Italy, in 1955, since 1980 Gruber has led a number of travel/study groups, treks, and expeditions in North and South America, in the Sahara, and above all in Central Asia (Hindu Kush, the Karakoram, and the Himalayan region). Besides this work, he is a photographer, author, and lecturer.

SIGI HUPFAUER

A German climber born in 1941, Hupfauer began to climb at the age of ten. Besides opening new routes on the Alps, including the super direct route up the north face of the Eiger in 1966, he has made over seventy-five expeditions around the world. He has climbed eight 8,000s—including Nanga Parbat, which he scaled in 1988 after twenty years of trying, and Manaslu, Everest, Shisha Pangma, Gasherbrum I and II, and Cho Oyu. The long list of his climbs includes eighty-five 5,000s, forty-five 6,000s, and ten 7,000s.

DEAN JOHNSTON

A New Zealander and amateur climber, Johnston is the chairman of the Canterbury Mountaineering Club.

HANS KAMMERLANDER

Born in Valle Aurina, Italy, in 1956, at the age of eight Kammerlander set off in pursuit of the only thing that made him feel free—the mountains. He became an alpine guide in 1979, and in the winter—when he is not climbing—he works as a ski instructor. Reinhold Messner took him along on his climbs of Cho Oyu, on Gasherbrum I and II, on Annapurna, and on Dhaulagiri. Then came Lhotse, Makalu, Cerro Torre (scaled in just seventeen hours), Nanga Parbat, and a number of other exploits, including an attempt to descend Everest on skis. His most recent achievement, in 1992, was the ascent and descent of the four slopes of the Matterhorn in 23 hours and 26 minutes. He boasts eight 8,000s, has climbed 1,300 mountains around the world, has opened twenty new routes, and made fifty solo climbs.

THOMAS KITCHIN

A Canadian photographer now living in Vancouver, Kitchen is well known for his wildlife photography. He contributes to the leading magazines in the field around the world. His photographs appear in just about every publication that deals with Canada. He is also highly regarded as an advertising photographer.

GERARD KOSICKI

A French photographer, Kosicki was born in Grenoble in 1955. His major layouts, magazine covers, and work of all sorts for the press and advertising are as famous internationally as they are in France. He is especially highly regarded for his photographs of mountains and all sorts of climbing.

MARCO MAJRANI

Born in Milan in 1952, Majrani took a degree in earth sciences and has worked as a photographer and journalist for over ten years. His work—especially in the areas of geography and the environment—has been published in a number of different nature magazines in Italy. He has taken part, as a geographer and journalist, in seven scientific and mountain climbing expeditions to the Andes and the Himalayas, and has also climbed previously unscaled peaks. He has also organized ten naturalistic expeditions to Chile, Argentina, Mexico, Costa Rica, Iceland, Australia, and New Zealand.

Born in 1962 in Trentino, Italy, Manica began to climb at the age of fifteen, following the established routes of the Dolomites and blazing new routes of his own. Thereafter, he climbed primarily in Patagonia—he was the first to scale the north wall of Cerro Pier Giorgio, the west wall of the Central Tower, and the North and South Towers of the Paine.

HEINZ MARIACHER

Born in Wörgl, in the Tyrol, Mariacher lives in Carezza, Italy. He is one of the best known climbers in the world. In the seventies, he was famous for his versions of the great routes of the Dolomites, many of which he did solo. From 1979 on, he worked on the south wall of Marmolada, where he put his signature on routes such as Abrakadabra and Moderne Zeiten. Today, he chiefly climbs for sport with his girlfriend, the renowned climber Luisa Jovane.

MARCO MILANI

Born in Turin in 1961, Milani is a climber and photographer with extensive experience on the major walls in the Alps. He is a climbing instructor, and has made expeditions to Pakistan, India, the U.S., Norway, and Morocco. He has made a number of successful climbs in the Alps and outside of Europe. Currently, he is a full-time mountain photographer and also works in public relations for athletic gear.

COLIN MONTEATH

A photographer and an expert author on the polar regions and on mountains in general, Monteath lives in Christchurch, New Zealand. He has participated in more than forty expeditions to Antarctica in the past twenty years, with voyages to the Transantarctic Mountains, expeditions on the active volcano, Mount Erebus, and a descent into the crater; he has also made a number of climbs in New Zealand, on the Andes, in the Pamirs in the former Soviet Union, and in the Tibetan, Nepalese, and Indian Himalayas. His work is published in leading nature magazines.

PATRICK MORROW

A professional photographer, but an adventurer by vocation, Morrow lives in Kimberly, British Columbia. He has explored the world with his camera and notebook for more than a decade and has reported on such exotic places as the African savannah, the jungles of Irian Jaya, and the mountains of Antarctica, and has published his work in a number of magazines in Europe and North America. He has published many books of his photography. In 1982, he reached the summit of Everest, thus becoming the first human to climb the highest peak on all seven continents.

GIOVANNI PIDELLO

Born in Turin in 1964, Pidello has worked professionally as a photographer since 1985. After some activity in the field of advertising and aerial photography, he has specialized in mountain photography. His love of the mountains has led him to scale peaks in the Alps tirelessly, both on walls and with skis. His photography has been published by a number of magazines around the world.

MICHEL PIOLA

Born in Switzerland in 1958, Piola is an alpine guide, an architect, and a teacher of physical education in Geneva. He is an expert on the great routes of the Alps, and his name is chiefly linked to Mont Blanc, where he has blazed a number of new routes on rock. He has also blazed five new routes up the north wall of the Eiger and one on the Matterhorn. He is an enthusiastic winter climber and big wall climber, and has taken part in expeditions to Greenland, the Himalayas, Patagonia, and Borneo. He contributes to a number of specialty magazines in Europe and has authored guides to Mont Blanc.

Library of Congress Cataloging-in Publication Data

Ardito, Stefano.
    Peaks of glory : climbing the worlds highest
mountains / Stefano Ardito.
      p. cm.
    ISBN 1-56566-045-5
    1. Mountaineering--History. I. Title
GV199.89.A73   1993
796.5'22--dc20   93-11320
                       CIP

CHRISTOPHE PROFIT

Born in 1961 in France, Profit is an alpine guide in the Compagnie des Guides de Chamonix. He has made a great many prestigious climbs, including the ascent of Mount Thule at the North Pole. His specialties are "enchaînements," solo, at great altitude. Among his best-known climbs are the north walls of Droites, Talèfre, and the Grands Jorasses, the first winter solo climb up the Eiger, in ten hours, the winter "trilogy" (Grandes Jorasses, Eiger, and Matterhorn in forty-two hours) in 1989 and 1990, attempts on the south wall of Lhotse, and in 1991 the ascent of K2 by the northwest wall (a new route) with Pierre Béghin. This photograph, taken by his fellow climber, shows him on the summit.

RENE ROBERT

Born in Briançon, France, in 1961, Robert now lives in Chamonix. He first debuted as a climber at the age of thirteen. Until 1985, he repeated the "classic" climbs of the Alps: Mont Blanc, Grandes Jorasses, Droites, Drus. Later, he took part in climbs in the Himalayas: Tent Peak, Everest (Nepal and Tibet), Pumori, and Latok 1. His love for photography and for mountaineering turned into a profession. "Mountain climbers are completely mad, just like all of the photographers that I have ever met. It is the basis for an excellent relationship."

JOHN ROSKELLEY

Born in Spokane, Washington, where he lives with his family, Roskelley grew up in close contact with nature. He began to climb at the age of sixteen, and eventually became one of the most famous and active American climbers in the Himalayas. He has climbed on K2, Makalu, Dhaulagiri, Nanda Devi, and the Towers of Uli Biaho. "I am still hard at the game," he admits. "The only alternative is to get a real job, and that's too risky."

GALEN ROWELL

Born in 1940 in Berkeley, California, where he still lives, Rowell is a respected climber and a renowned professional photographer. At the age of sixteen, he began to climb in the Yosemite Valley, blazing more than a hundred new routes. He has made over thirty-five expeditions to the mountains of Nepal, India, Pakistan, China, Tibet, Africa, Alaska, Canada, Siberia, New Zealand, Norway, and Patagonia. He has climbed Everest, K2, Gasherbrum II, Cholatse, and the Towers of Trango.

MARK SHAPIRO

Born near Toronto, Canada, in 1947, Shapiro now lives near Verbier, Switzerland. He began as an amateur photographer in 1970 and then moved to Europe; in 1974, he sold his first work, and his photography has become increasingly popular since then. His snow photography appears regularly in magazines.

JANEZ SKOK

Born in 1961, Skok now lives in Ljubljana, Slovenia, in the former Yugoslavia. He holds a degree in economics, but his real love is photography. He has been a mountain climber since 1976, and he specializes in mountain photography, contributing to the leading European magazines in the field. He has taken part in a number of expeditions to the Karakoram, Kashmir, and Patagonia, and has made a number of successful extreme climbs.

PASCAL TOURNAIRE

Born in 1959 in Paris, Tournaire has been climbing mountains since he was fifteen. He became a journalist in 1979. He works extensively as a reporter and photographer for the leading specialty magazines in France. He first went to the Himalayas in 1988—he has scaled the south wall of Annapurna and the north wall of Everest, as well as the Vinson Massif, Mount McKinley, Kilimanjaro, and Aconcagua.

CÉSAR PÉREZ DE TUDELA

A Spanish lawyer, but first and foremost a mountain climber, Pérez de Tudela is famous for his climbing over the past thirty-five years as well as for his writing about mountain climbing (for the press, radio, and television). He made the first winter climb on the west wall of Naranjo de Bulnes and has participated in many expeditions outside of Europe: Cerro Torre, Aconcagua, Cotopaxi, Mount McKinley, Ruwenzori, Annapurna, and Everest.

MARC FRANCIS TWIGHT

Born in California in 1961, Twight now lives in Chamonix. In 1984, he made a number of successful solo climbs on the Alps and attracted the attention of the climbing world. This paved the way for his participation in Himalayan expeditions on Kangtega, Nuptse, Nanga Parbat, Everest, Pik Kommunizm (or Peak of Communism), Khan Tengri, and to blazing new routes on Kongma-Tse and Lingtren Peak; he also made a solo climb of the direct route up the north wall of Kusum Kanguru. He is a photographer and a writer, and has worked for the leading magazines in Europe and America, as well as on film documentaries.

MARIO VERIN

Verin, a member of the Italian Academic Alpine Club, is also an alpine instructor. Since 1988 he has worked exclusively as a photographer and journalist, contributing to a number of European mountaineering magazines and a number of Italian periodicals. He has spent a great deal of time in Africa and the Middle East.

HEINZ ZAK

Born in Wörgl, in the Tyrol, in 1958, Zak began climbing at the age of fifteen. His passion for rock climbing led him to make his first difficult ascents on the local peaks, the Wetterstein and the Karwendel, where he traversed the principal ridges for some twenty-five miles and did the thirty-six peaks, solo, in seventy-two hours. He has also found new climbing territory in Australia, China, and Peru. As a rock climber, he is above Grade X, and as a solo climber, Grade IX. He is also known throughout the world as a mountain photographer.